THE MARGARET BOYLES

BARGELLO WORKBOOK

OTHER BOOKS BY MARGARET BOYLES

Needlepoint Stitchery
Bargello: An Explosion in Color
American Indian Needlepoint Workbook
    (based on material by W. Ben Hunt
    and J. F. "Buck" Burshears)

THE MARGARET BOYLES

BARGELLO WORKBOOK

A Collection of Original Designs

MACMILLAN PUBLISHING CO., INC.
New York

COLLIER MACMILLAN PUBLISHERS
London

This book is for my mother,
Margaret James Webb,
who will enjoy it almost as much
as I enjoyed writing it.

Copyright © 1976 by Margaret Boyles

Macmillan Publishing Co., Inc.
866 Third Avenue, New York, N.Y. 10022
Collier Macmillan Canada, Ltd.

Library of Congress Cataloging in Publication Data
Boyles, Margaret.
   The Margaret Boyles bargello workbook.

   1. Canvas embroidery—Patterns. I. Title.
TT778.C3B678   746.4′4   76-6991
ISBN 0-02-514330-1

First Printing 1976

Designed by Margaret Dodd

Photography by the author

Printed in the United States of America

CONTENTS

INTRODUCTION

Bargello, by definition, is a specialized, counted canvas embroidery characterized by long upright stitches and repeated geometric designs. These range from the best-loved simple flame patterns to the most complicated of Florentines with stitches of various lengths. For generations these old favorites have been used and reused, changing little as time passed. Occasionally a flash of ingenuity or a fresh approach to color and composition has appeared, but by and large the patterns have remained the same. The old designs are lovely and have a classic appeal that adapts to changing trends, and explains their enduring quality.

It is perhaps because this classic beauty is so great that new possibilities for using the designs have been so little explored. This book is one designer's effort to take a new approach to Bargello and Bargello-type canvas embroidery. Not all the designs presented herein are conventional Bargello, but all have roots in the traditional embroidery. It is one of the designer's functions to establish new lines of thought and show innovative use of time-honored techniques. The broad spectrum of designs, therefore, includes true Bargello, intriguing Four-way, combined patterns, and a selection of Bargello-like embroideries on canvas.

To give the reader an insight into the development of the compositions, the sequence of designs begins with two easy traditional Bargello pillows worked on large-mesh canvas, demonstrating the fact that even the easiest of patterns is beautiful when worked correctly in well-chosen colors. A novice will find the beginner pillows within the scope of his ability.

Four-way or mitered Bargello was explored very superficially in this country as early as the eighteenth century. Of the early pieces several handsome rugs featuring mitered designs as borders point in the direction of today's exciting Four-way designs. Actually, most traditional Bargello can be worked Four-way with astonishing results. Even a simple single-line design becomes an intriguing new pattern when the canvas is divided into four triangles and the line worked within the sections. This principle is illustrated with another easy pattern in monochromatic color on large-mesh canvas. This easy beginning forms the basis of an understanding of the mechanics of Four-way, and it is natural to progress to more elaborate designs. Some are veritable kaleidoscopes, others are soft and delicate; some are more advanced than others, but all are intriguing to work.

In this age, in which we live with surprising combinations of pattern in fashion as well as in home furnishings, it seems natural to expect to find such composition in embroidery. The patchwork look is much offered, but too often it lacks the design expertise to lift it out of the old "leftover" look. Far better to combine just a few patterns into a compatible whole, uniting them in scale, color, and feeling. The combinations may include true Bargello and Four-way in surprising mixes until the total design is viewed. The look is completely new, fun to work, and a pleasure to display. After trying the combinations in this book, many a reader will be working out original compositions.

Though they are not Bargello in the strictest sense of the word, many of the designs are a counted type of canvas embroidery so like Bargello that for lack of a better word or classification they are simply called Bargello-type embroideries. They are a natural outgrowth of the design process, and develop in many ways. Their use broadens the possibilities for creating an entirely new look for canvas embroidery. These are the most interesting to work—patterns change, colors interact— no chance for boredom to set in.

It must be obvious that I enjoyed designing the Bargello for this book; I hope that the reader will find equal pleasure in re-creating the needlepoint.

Happy stitching!

Margaret Boyles

THE DESIGNS

BEGINNER PILLOW

A glance through the pages of this book affirms that Bargello design can often be very complex both in color and pattern. This little pillow is included both as a beginner project and as proof that simple design and good color also add up to a handsome piece. The design is a variation of one of the most loved and used lines. The canvas is an easy-to-see and -work #10 interlocking mono and the yarn is Persian in five blending antique golds. The addition of the Gobelin stitch border and the fat tassels pull all elements together into a pleasing composition.

Color changes for this pillow are no problem. Any five graduated shades of one color will produce a good-looking monotone effect similar to the one shown. Contrasting colors may also be used with good results, for this is a very versatile design.

FINISHED SIZE: 10″ x 12″.
MATERIALS:
- #10 white interlocking mono canvas approximately 14″ x 16″.
- #18 tapestry needle.
- Persian yarn as follows: 511, Pecan, 2 skeins; 521, Earth, 2 skeins; 531, Empire Gold, 2 skeins; 541, Pale Gold, 2 skeins; 455, Yellow White, 2 skeins.
- Half-yard appropriate fabric for pillow back.

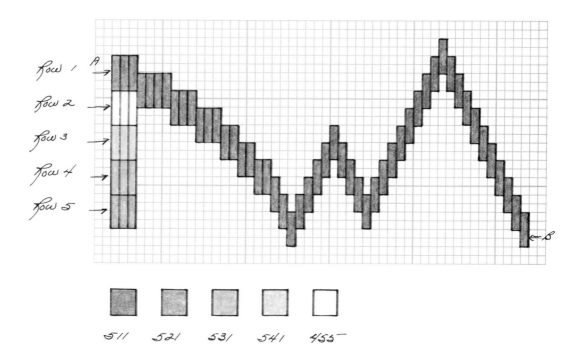

Row 1 A
Row 2
Row 3
Row 4
Row 5

511 521 531 541 455

NOTE: If pillow is to be finished with tassels as shown, an additional skein of 511 Pecan will be needed. Make tassels following instructions included with directions for completing pillows on page 118.

NOTE: Use full three-ply yarn throughout except for back stitches between rows of Gobelin in border. For these stitches separate yarn and use two-ply.

STEP: Entire design is a 4-2 step.

INSTRUCTIONS: Tape canvas and mark with lines "A" and "B" for simple Bargello as in Chart 1 on page 111.

Begin row 1 at "A" in center of canvas with darkest shade of yarn in needle. Counting stitches, work across chart to "B." End yarn. Attach again at "A" and work to left side of canvas, repeating portion of row previously worked.

The chart shows only one complete row, as all rows are a repetition of first. Color blocks marked with row numbers are key to color sequence. Only first row must be divided to center it. Subsequent rows can be worked from right to left all the way across the canvas.

Attach lightest color at left edge and repeat pattern for Row 2. Repeat, following correct color shading, until six complete rows have been worked. Point at which lowest stitches of Row 6 touch thread is the bottom edge of pattern. Continue working downward, but do not work below this edge. Use compensating stitches to square off edge where necessary.

Turn canvas around so that bottom half is unfinished. Keeping color sequence correct, finish other half of piece. This portion will require ten complete rows plus partial rows to square edge.

Finish edges with three rows of Gobelin stitch border worked over four threads. First row should be color 541, second row 531, final row 511. If small white portions of threads show between rows of Gobelin border, work a row of back stitch between rows in yarn to match. This will cover white and add dimension to the Gobelin stitches.

Block and assemble pillow according to instructions on page 117.

HERALDIC PILLOW

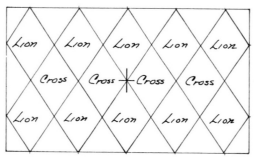

+ denotes center mesh or square

Heraldic symbols and the royal colors adapt to Bargello for an unusual pillow. The lion rampant and the cross are simplified but retain their original character, while the vivid hues could have been taken from an old coat of arms. Fat tassels at the corners add elegance.

While the design is most effective in the colors shown, another color can be substituted for the blue background to fit other needs. The white, gold, and red shown will coordinate with many other colors.

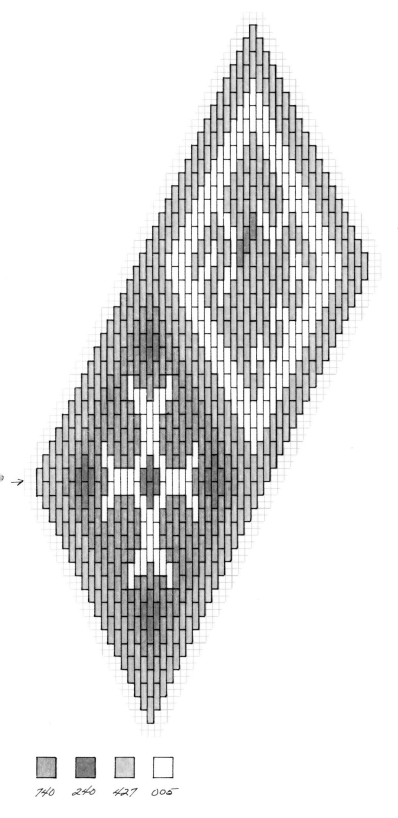

FINISHED SIZE: 10½" x 14".
MATERIALS:
- #12 white mono canvas approximately 15" x 18".
- #20 tapestry needle.
- Persian yarn as follows: 740, Blue, 3 skeins; 240, Red, 1 skein; 427, Gold, 2 skeins; 005, White, 2 skeins.
- One-half yard appropriate fabric for pillow back.

NOTE: If pillow is to be finished with tassels, as shown, one additional skein of 427, Gold will be needed. Make tassels following instructions on page 118.

NOTE: Use yarn full three-ply throughout.

STEP: Design is a 4-2 step.

INSTRUCTIONS: Divide and mark canvas for simple Bargello as in Chart 1 on page 111.

With gold yarn place stitch "A" at the crossing of the dividing lines. This position is indicated by the upright cross on the center of the layout chart. Using the layout chart for guidance and the color diagram for stitch count, work the three rows of gold diamonds. There are five diamonds across in the upper and lower rows. (These form the four in the center row.)

Again checking with the layout chart, fill in the diamonds with the appropriate figures. Note that lions are in top and bottom rows, crosses in center. All lions are on white background, all crosses on blue.

Fill in partial diamonds at edges with solid blue brick stitch to form a straight edge. Work blue four mesh beyond outlines of diamonds.

Block and construct pillow following directions on page 117.

740   240   427   005

PALE BLUE PICTURE FRAME

A favorite snapshot shows off to good advantage in a delicately shaded petit point frame worked in an uncomplicated Bargello design. Blending shades of blue with the special sheen of cotton embroidery floss are worked on #22 canvas for this softly padded frame.

Commercially packaged frames to be covered in needlepoint or other fabrics are available, but this one is entirely hand made. It is an easy project, requiring few materials—the needlepoint, heavy cardboard, rubber cement, and a handful of dacron fiber.

FINISHED SIZE: 5¾″ x 5¾″.
MATERIALS:
- #22 cream mono canvas approximately 10″ x 10″.
- #24 tapestry needle.
- DMC six-strand embroidery floss as follows: 813, Medium Blue, 4 skeins; 3325, Blue, 2 skeins; 775, Pale Blue, 3 skeins.
- Heavy cardboard approximately 5¾″ square.

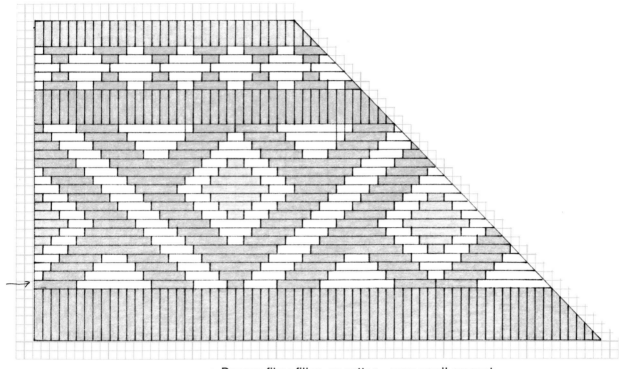

9 →

813   3325   775

- Dacron fiber filler, or cotton—very small amount.
- Small scrap of fabric to cover back of frame.
- Rubber cement or thick craft glue.

NOTE: Use all six strands of the embroidery floss for the Bargello. Work with an even tension so the stitches will be smooth. If one strand of floss separates from the rest lift the stitch with the needle and smooth it back into place.

STEP: This design departs slightly from typical Bargello patterns in that it uses stitches lying both horizontally and vertically on the canvas. Since stitches vary in length there is no definite step pattern. Follow chart carefully until design is established on canvas.

INSTRUCTIONS: Tape canvas and mark with all four guidelines as for Four-way Bargello on page 111. The chart shows only one-half of the side of the frame. Establish pattern of darkest blue diagonals by following chart from "A" to the miter line, which is the corner of frame. Attach thread again at "A" and repeat chart to left edge of canvas to complete one side of frame. Repeat to form square.

The frame will need very little blocking. Slight steaming (see Blocking, page 115) should be sufficient. Trim canvas borders to one-half inch on all edges. Remove unworked canvas center, leaving half-inch borders also. Slash canvas to corners along miter lines and turn to inside to form a neat edge for frame.

Cut heavy cardboard 5½" square. Cut center opening to exact measurement of needlepoint. Cement edges of needlepoint to opening of frame. Allow to dry. Working on one of the outside frame edges at a time, place dacron filling into frame and cement needlepoint in place along back edge of cardboard. Miter corners to make as neat as possible.

Cut another cardboard to size of frame. Cover with fabric. Place picture between frame and covered back sandwich-fashion and glue back to frame. Attach a fabric-covered easel to back.

FRENCH PEASANT EYEGLASS CASE

Six-strand embroidery floss on #22 canvas works up into a small eyeglass case that looks more like a French cotton fabric than Bargello. It takes a careful combination of all elements—the tiny repeat design, the fine mesh of the canvas, the sheen of the cotton thread, the choice and shading of colors—to achieve this look. It is particularly lovely for an accessory like this.

Although the canavs is #22—really petit point size—the Bargello stitches save it from being a tedious project, and it can be finished in a reasonably short time. As a matter of fact this kind of piece is an excellent introduction to working on the finer canvas sizes.

The little flower in this design is the same as the one in the Flower Bargello Pillow on page 31. Worked in different colors and placed differently on the canvas, it is a perfect example of the many ways the designs in this book can be adapted to uses other than those shown in the finished projects.

The golds used in the embroidery of this piece are compatible with many background colors in addition to the navy blue shown. Others to try could be black, dark green, old red, brown, rust, and deep rose.

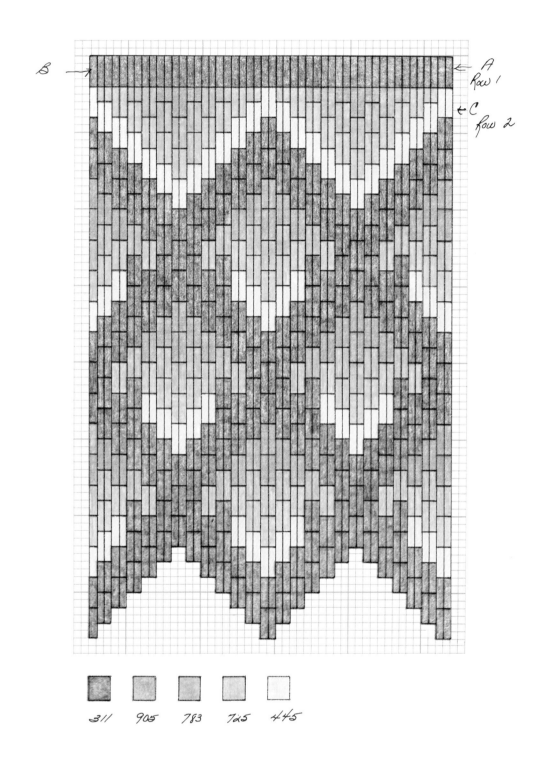

B →
A ←
Row 1
← C
Row 2

311   905   783   725   445

FINISHED SIZE: 2¼″ x 6¼″.

MATERIALS:
- #22 cream mono canvas approximately 8″ x 9″.
- #24 tapestry needle.
- DMC six-strand embroidery floss as follows: 311, Blue, 3 skeins; 1 skein each: 905, Green; 783, Medium Gold; 725, Light Gold; 445, Yellow.
- Small piece of velveteen or corduroy in coordinating color for lining.

NOTE: Use all six strands of embroidery floss just as it is skeined. Keep tension even on all strands as work proceeds so that stitches will be smooth.
If one strand loosens lift stitch with the needle and smooth thread with finger.

STEP: Pattern is a 4-2 step with all stitches in groups of two.

INSTRUCTIONS: Prepare canvas. The front and back of the case are identical. The chart shows either front or back full width, but only three repeats of the floral design. To complete the depth of the case it will be necessary to repeat the chart until seven rows of flowers are worked.

Begin Row 1 at "A" about 1 inch in from top and side edges of right side of canvas. Work across row from "A" to "B" and repeat back from "B" to "A" to complete the entire width of the case.

Work Row 2 beginning at "C" as indicated on the chart. Fill in gold border, following the chart for guidance in color placement. Work down from top until seven rows of flowers have been completed. Fill in lower edges with that portion of design needed to square edge.

Block (see page 115). Trim excess canvas from needlepoint, leaving a half-inch seam allowance on all edges. Cut lining to size, using trimmed Bargello as a guide. Fold lining in half, right sides together, and seam bottom and side. Trim seam allowance, but do not turn lining.

With steam iron carefully press seam allowances of needlepoint to inside. Beginning at bottom edge and working from the right side, whip case together as far as the corner. Insert the lining into the folded case and continue joining to top edge. Turn seam allowance at top of lining to inside and whip to the top of the case.

COLONIAL FLAME PILLOW

The dominant design element in this pillow is obviously color—color so important that it is almost forgotten that a single line establishes the pattern. The alternating stitches at the top and bottom of the flames bring about a beautiful blending of colors as they shade from light to dark. To play up this effect, the yarns used are carefully chosen to include values of blue, green, and red, dyed to blend beautifully.

At this time of heightened excitement about the national Bicentennial celebration it is interesting to note that this serrated flame design was an American colonial favorite, often worked in color as brilliant, but not as permanent as this. Fading and oxidation have usually softened the early dyes to the subtle hues now associated with eighteenth-century decoration and embroidery.

However much the extraordinarily bright colors of the pillow are admired, admittedly they will not fit into every decorating scheme.

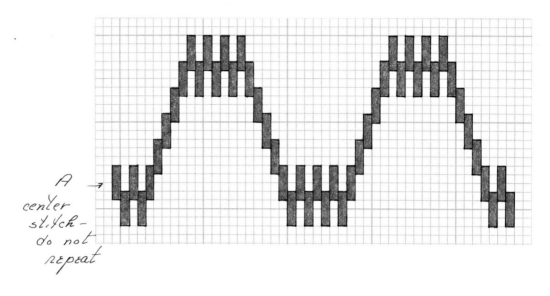

A → center stitch — do not repeat

The versatile design adapts to a monochromatic or two-color theme easily. The range of golds used for the Pomegranate and Ribbon Pillow on page 48 or the French blues of the Kaleidoscope Panel on page 53 are two of the many possibilities. Number 10 canvas and a 12-inch size combine with the fascination of watching the colors blend to make this a project finished almost too quickly.

SIZE: 12″ x 12″.

MATERIALS:

- #10 white interlocking canvas approximately 16″ x 16″.
- #18 tapestry needle.
- Less than 1 skein of each color each is required, since there are so many colors involved. Use Persian yarn as follows:
  Greens: 520, Hunter Green; 510, Medium Green; 545, Avocado; 550, Antique Lime; 565, Yellow Green; 580, Yellow Lime.
  Blues: 740, Dark Blue; 742, True Blue; 752, Medium Blue; 754, Light Medium Blue; 756, Summer Blue.
  Reds: 240, Cranberry; R10, True Red; 242, Red; 958, Dark Orange; 960, Burnt Orange; 970, Light Orange; 450, Yellow; 458, Daffodil; 050, Black.
  One-half yard appropriate fabric for pillow back.

NOTE: Use yarn fully-ply just as it comes from the skein. If coverage is not adequate see page 105 for help in solving this problem.

STEP: The entire pattern is a 4-1 step.

INSTRUCTIONS: Tape the canvas and mark with the two basic lines "A" and "B" for traditional Bargello.

Since the design is a repeat of only one line, the chart shows just that one line. Begin at the center of the canvas with the darkest shade of red. Starting at stitch "A" on the chart, count the row from the center of the canvas to the right edge. End the yarn and attach again at the center. Now count the row to the left. All succeeding rows can now be worked all the way across the canvas.

The color sequence is to be worked as follows. Row 1 is color 240 (already worked). Work downward, using one row each of the reds in the following order: R10, 242, 958, 960, 970, 450, and 458. Work one row of black.

Follow with the blue family in this order: 740, 742, 752, 754, 756. Work one row of black. This is the last full row at bottom of pillow.

Turn the canvas and work one row of black followed by the greens in this order: 580, 565, 550, 545, 510, and 520. Work the final row of black. Fill remaining spaces at edge with the blue family, working from light to dark as necessary to square off edge. Turn canvas and fill in spaces below blue rows with the green family, working down from the darkest hue as needed to square edge.

Finish edge with a Gobelin border as follows: One row black with stitches over two threads; one row color 960 over three threads; 242 over three threads; 240 worked four threads wide; and a final row of black over three threads. With a single strand of yarn work a row of back stitch in matching colors between the Gobelin rows.

Block and construct pillow according to directions on page 117.

EIGHTEENTH-CENTURY CANDLE SCREEN

This graceful reproduction of an eighteenth-century candle screen deserved special treatment and its tiny frame was a challenge, for the piece to go in it must be appropriate in scale as well as in feeling. In keeping with the reproduction's period, the design is an adaptation of an old Bargello favorite updated with color and new interpretation.

The 4" x 5" size of the frame dictated that a fine-mesh canvas be used to keep the Bargello stitches in scale with the size of the candle screen. Number 22 canvas was chosen, and though at first it seems to be very delicate, the long Bargello stitches relieve the work from any tendency to be tedious. It is surprising how quickly the piece is finished.

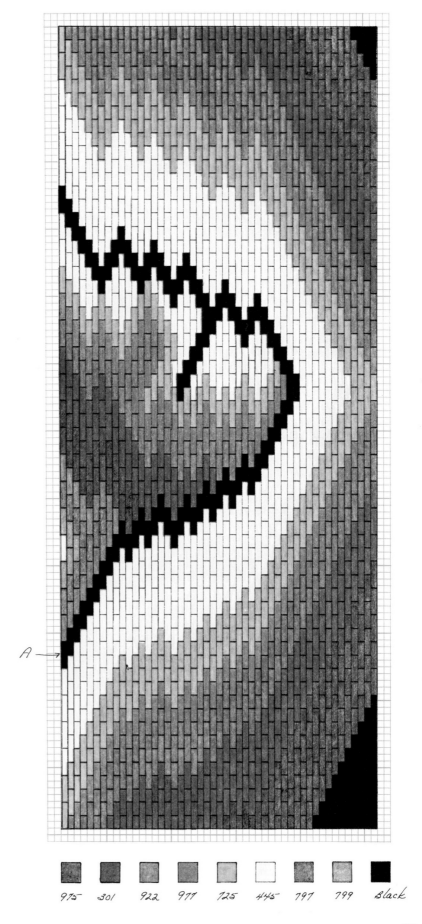

A →

| 975 | 301 | 922 | 977 | 725 | 445 | 797 | 799 | Black |

The best choice of thread for #22 canvas is six-strand embroidery floss, the glowing colors of which enhance the gleam of the rubbed mahogany finish of the screen.

The candle screen is shown courtesy of the manufacturer, Plain and Fancy, Mathews, Va. 23109. It is available in needlework shops and department stores nationally.

Carnation Design for Candle Screen

The carnation pattern, a great favorite in the late seventeenth and entire eighteenth centuries, has survived on a few chair seats prized by museums in the United States and Great Britain. The cushions utilize the design as a typical Bargello repeat worked in bright colors. Most are worked in a combination of silks and wool, and it is interesting to note that most contain very irregularly counted carnations. The embroidress of days gone by did not enjoy our supply of fine needlework materials, and the uneven weave of her canvas often accounts in part for the charming variations found in one piece.

For the candle screen a single carnation was placed against a shaded background. The motif can also be used as a repeat on a solid ground for a larger project.

FINISHED SIZE: 4″ x 5″.
MATERIALS:
- #22 cream mono canvas.
- #24 tapestry needle.
- DMC six-strand embroidery floss as follows: One skein each Black; 975, Brown; 301, Rust; 922, Medium Rust; 977, Light Rust; 725, Gold; 445, Yellow; 797, Dark Blue; 799, Medium Blue.

NOTE: Use all six strands of embroidery floss. Keep an even tension on the strands so the stitches will be smooth. If one strand separates from the rest lift the stitch with the needle and adjust the tension so all are even.

STEP: Entire design is worked in a 4-2 step.

INSTRUCTIONS: Tape canvas. Mark center lines "A" and "B," following the instructions with Chart on page 111.

Begin by outlining the carnation in black. Make the first stitch—"A" on the chart—on the vertical line about 1¼″ below the center line. Work entire flower outline. Next fill in the blue calyx as on the diagram. Work remainder of carnation up from the blue so that shading is easier.

The shimmering background at first seems complicated, but is actually a series of rows worked around the carnation, following its shape and fading out from the lightest yellow to the darker hues. Begin by attaching the yellow at one side of the flower and working around it four times, following the black outline exactly. Continue with the other colors as shown on the chart, ending with the small number of black stitches in each corner.

The finished piece should need very little blocking. Freshen with steam, but be careful not to rest the iron on the embroidery. Stretch on the hardboard back of the frame and tape securely into place. Insert in frame and assemble screen according to directions supplied with it.

CHRISTMAS ORNAMENTS

It seems as though needlepoint is popping up everywhere. Now appear Bargello ornaments for the Christmas tree. Since the shapes of many Bargello motifs are similar to those of many traditional decorations of the season, they translate readily into attractive conversation-piece ornaments. Eight designs are shown, but after several have been made following the charts, the reader will most likely be working out individual variations, for the possibilities are endless.

Traditional Christmas colors have been used on #14 canvas—two bright greens, gold, and red. The canvas is fine enough to allow for a reasonable amount of detail, but large enough to allow one to make several ornaments in an evening. Substitute colors and make custom ornaments to coordinate with other holiday colors.

18

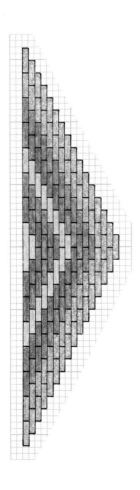

FINISHED SIZE: Ornaments vary because of design differences, but most are approximately 2½″ to 3½″.

MATERIALS:
- #14 white mono canvas, 6″ square for each ornament.
- 20 tapestry needle.
- For eight ornaments 1 skein each: 559, Brilliant Green; 569, Apple Green; R-50, Dark Red; 440, Topaz.
- Small amount of polyester fiber.
- Four skeins cotton embroidery floss in bright gold for tassels.

NOTE: Separate yarn and work with two-ply.

INSTRUCTIONS: For each ornament make two pieces, following chart for chosen design. Steam the two pieces. Trim canvas to one-half inch. With steam iron press seam allowance to inside, folding as close as possible to the Bargello stitches.

Following the instructions on page 118, make a tassel, using a cardboard 1¾″ wide. Also make a twisted cord two inches long to be used as a loop for hanging the ornament. Attach these to one side of the steamed canvas in the proper position.

Using a double strand of yarn in the color matching the outside row of Bargello, and beginning at the top, whip the two pieces together. When the seam is closed except for about an inch, stuff lightly and continue stitching to the top.

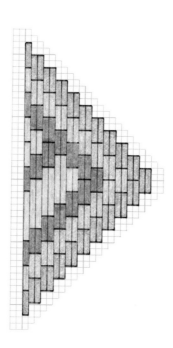

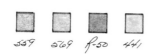

559   569   R-50   441

KEY-CHAIN TAG

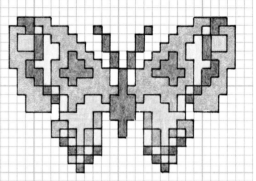

A cute little project is a tag to attach to an inexpensive key chain. This one originally had a plastic $100 bill attached to the metal ring, which now holds the Bargello and needlepoint tag. This tag is slightly stuffed with polyester fiber for bulk, but can be finished flat if that look is preferred. Also there are several options available in planning the tag—both sides can match, or one side can be initialed, the other display the butterfly.

FINISHED SIZE: 2½″ x 3½″ at widest points.

MATERIALS:
- #14 white mono canvas approximately 5″ x 8″.
- Small amounts (much less than half a skein) of the colors shown on the charts or colors preferred.
- Initial side: Several yards each: 756, Summer Blue; 395, Light Blue; 405, Copper.
- Butterfly: Several yards each: 005, White; 754, Light Medium Blue; 458, Daffodil; 405, Copper; 756, Summer Blue.
- #20 tapestry needle.
- A tiny handful of polyester filling.

NOTE: Work both the Bargello and the tent stitch with two-ply.

INSTRUCTIONS: Make two pieces, either both alike or the two different designs coordinating background color. If the butterfly is to be used work only the outer row of Bargello. Then center and work in tent stitch.

Work the initial side as shown. Plan correct letter on graph paper and work in tent stitch centered in the tag.

Steam the two pieces. Trim canvas to one-half inch. With steam iron press seam allowances to inside, folding as close as possible to Bargello stitches.

Using a double strand of matching yarn, whip the two pieces together, beginning at the top. When the seam is closed except for about one inch, stuff lightly, then continue stitching to the top. Attach key chain to top with the same strand of yarn. If a flat tag is preferred, omit the filler.

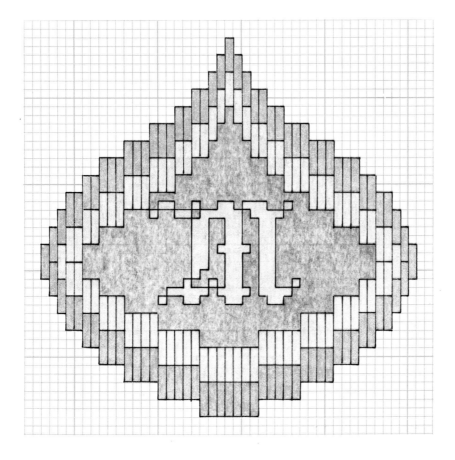

ETHNIC EMBROIDERY EYEGLASS CASE

COLORWAY #3

COLORWAY #2

In the exploration of the origins of embroidery one is often surprised to find the same type of designs developing in many countries and being identified with many national groups. The stylized flower worked into the Bargello diamonds of this eyeglass case is typical of many found in old embroideries of the Scandinavian countries, central Europe, Russia, and the Balkans. These old patterns provide the designer inspiration for many new interpretations that adapt readily to Bargello.

This eyeglass case is generous in size to accommodate most modern glasses. Although it is worked on a fine mesh canvas it will be finished quickly for the design is fascinating, and the yarn smooth and easy to use.

FINISHED SIZE: 3″ x 6¼″.

MATERIALS:

- #18 white mono canvas approximately 9″ x 10″.
- #22 tapestry needle.
- Elsa Williams tapestry yarn as follows: One skein each: 104, Deep Pink; 105, Pale Pink; 402, Dark Green; 404, Light Green; 805, White.

- Colorway #2: One skein each: 303, Medium Gold; 304, Gold; 305, Pale Yellow Gold; 802, Deep Gray.

- Colorway #3: One skein each: 501, Navy; 504, Slate Blue; 505, Pale Blue; 305, Pale Yellow Gold; 805, White.

- Small piece velveteen or corduroy in coordinating color for lining.

NOTE: Use yarn full-ply as it comes from the skein. At first the yarn may look heavy or thick for the #18 canvas. The Williams yarn is very soft, with a smooth twist that creates a beautiful piece of Bargello. Used on this canvas the yarn produces closely packed stitches resembling satin stitch embroidery. The padding provided by the bulk of the yarn offers extra protection for the glasses.

STEP: This design does not fall into a typical Bargello step pattern. The stitches are vertical, varying in length from two to ten mesh. The symmetry within each diamond makes working easy once the dark-green outlines of the motifs are placed.

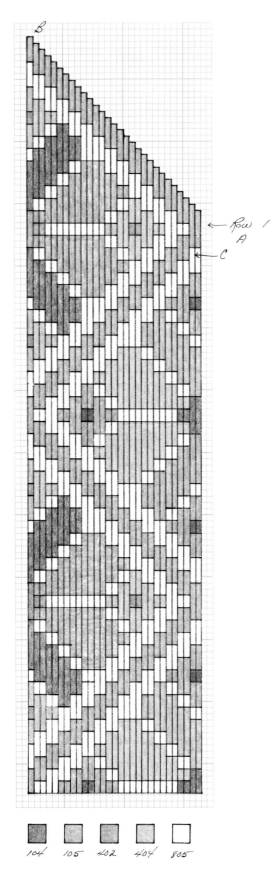

B

← Row 1
A

← C

104	105	402	404	805

INSTRUCTIONS: Prepare canvas and study the chart, noting that the stitches in Row 1 alternate in length over four and five mesh to provide a smooth edge to be turned back in finishing. Only Row 1 has this stitch variation.

The front and back of the case are identical. The chart shows one-half of either.

Row 1 should begin at the right side of the canvas at a point 3″ down from the top and 1½″ in from the side. Work Row 1 following the chart from "A" to "B" and back from "B" to "A" to complete top edge of one-half of case. Repeat to left side of canvas to finish row. Fasten yarn.

Attach dark-green yarn at point "C" on chart and, working from right to left, place the outlines of all diamonds. Fill in with the flower motifs, using the chart as a guide for color placement.

Block (see page 115). Using the completed needlepoint as a pattern, cut lining, allowing one-half inch for seam allowance on all sides. Fold lining in half, right sides together, and seam bottom and side. Trim seam allowances one-quarter inch, but do not turn lining.

Trim excess canvas from needlepoint, leaving one-half inch on all edges. With steam iron carefully press seam allowances to inside. Beginning at bottom edge and working from right side, whip the case together as far as the corner. Insert the lining into the folded case and continue sewing to the top edge. Turn seam allowance of top edge of lining to inside and whip to top of case.

BEGINNER FOUR-WAY PILLOW

The magic of four-way plotting turns an easy Bargello pattern into an exciting graphic design for this easy pillow top. The transition from a straight line pattern, as in the beginner pillow on page 2, is uncomplicated when the hints on working Four-way Bargello on page 107 are followed. Working techniques are basically the same as those used in traditional Bargello. Dividing the canvas into four triangles and working them so that all stitches radiate out from the center is the secret of the dramatic kaleidoscopelike designs.

When the canvas is a large mesh, like this #10 interlocking mono, it is best to keep the design simple. For this pillow a single large medalion is centered in each section and colorings are kept to monochromatic blends.

COLORWAY #2

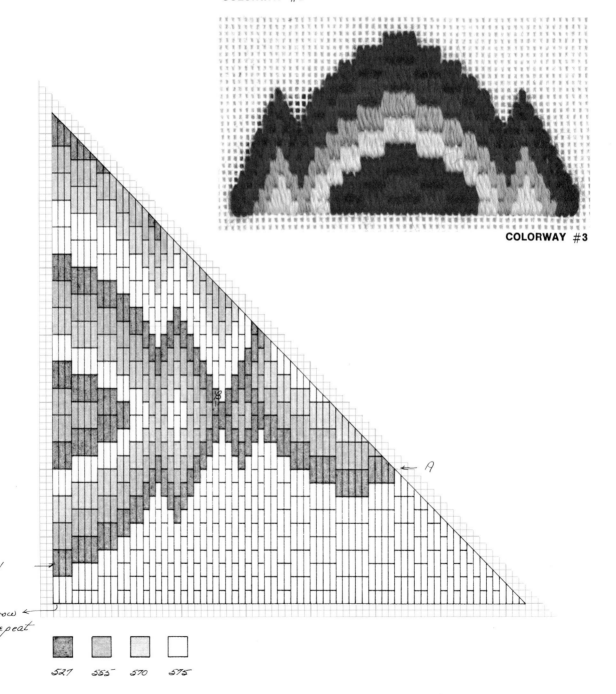
COLORWAY #3

Row 1

Center row
do not repeat

527   555   570   575

26

FINISHED SIZE: 14″ x 14″.
MATERIALS:
- #10 interlocking mono canvas approximately 18″ x 18″.
- #18 tapestry needle.
- Persian yarn as follows: 527, Moss, 2 skeins; 555, Green Giant, 2 skeins; 570, Celery Leaf, 1 skein; 575, Spring Pea Green, 3 skeins.

- Colorway #2: 334, Dark French Blue, 2 skeins; 330, Old Blue, 2 skeins; 756, Summer Blue, 1 skein; 395, Light Blue, 3 skeins.

- Colorway #3: 113, Dark Brown, 2 skeins; 405, Copper, 2 skeins; 257, Light Tan, 1 skein; 020, Natural, 3 skeins.

- One-half yard appropriate fabric for pillow back.

NOTE: Use yarn full three-ply throughout. If coverage is not adequate see hints for solving this problem on page 105.
STEP: This design is worked in a 4-2 step.

INSTRUCTIONS: Following the instructions on page 111, mark canvas for Four-way Bargello. Tape canvas.

On center vertical line measure in from bottom edge 2¼″. At this point work the group of darkest green stitches indicated as beginning of Row 1. Continue across chart to stitch "A" on the miter line. End yarn. Attach yarn again at center of row and work to miter line at opposite side, reading chart from center to "A" but working right to left. Place this dark-green row in remaining three quadrants. Check to ascertain that all rows meet at precisely the same point on the miter lines.

To avoid counting mesh to place the second dark-green row outlining the motif, attach yarn and begin to count at point "B" on chart. Complete this row in all four sections.

Beginning with palest shade (575), start working rows in toward center of piece. Follow the chart and work all four quarters all the way to the center. Next fill in large motifs and complete design. Work background of palest green, following stitch sequence established by design motif.

Block and construct pillow (see page 117).

This pillow in colors shown is available as a kit from Columbia–Minerva. Design used courtesy C–M.

BLUE INTRIGUE PILLOW

One of the reasons Bargello is so interesting is the fascination of watching the design take shape on the unmarked canvas. Four-way has an added intrigue in that the motifs meet along the miter lines to form unplanned designs. When plotted Four-way even a basic line design becomes an exciting kaleidoscopic pattern.

This blue-and-white pillow is typically interesting Four-way Bargello. The softly curved motifs stretch from miter line to miter line, forming intriguing new shapes where they join those of the adjacent quadrant. Four shades of blue team with white in a classic color scheme for an unconventional design. To accentuate the blue shapes the "background" was worked in all white, following the stitch pattern established by the colored motifs. Filling in these white portions in the shaded blues would create an entirely different feeling.

FINISHED SIZE: 14″ x 14″
MATERIALS:
- #14 white mono canvas approximately 18″ x 18″.
- #20 tapestry needle.
- Persian yarn in the following assortment: 742, True Blue, 2 skeins; 752, Medium Blue, 1 skein; 754, Light Medium Blue, 1 skein; 756, Summer Blue, 1 skein; 005, White, 3 skeins.

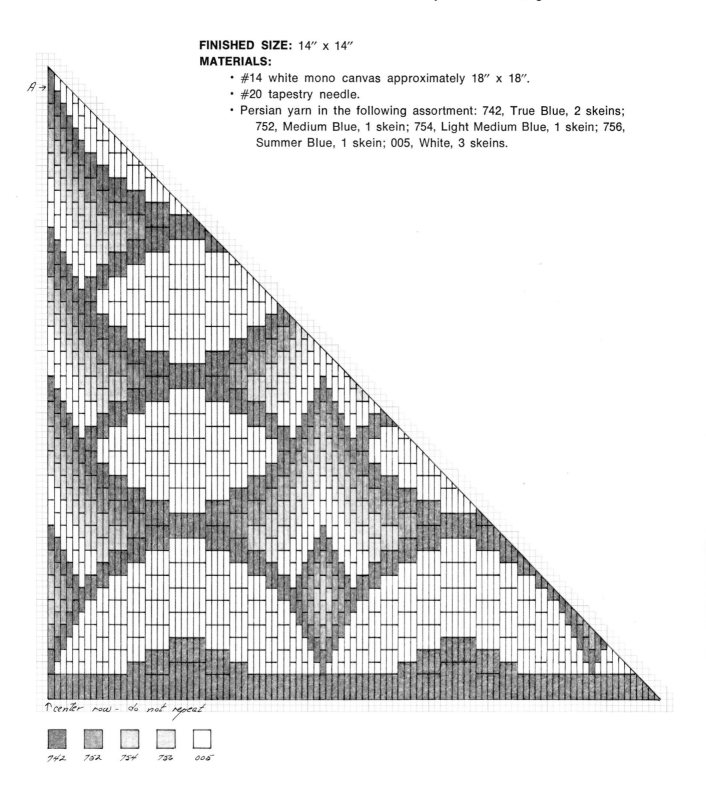

↑ center row - do not repeat

742   752   754   756   005

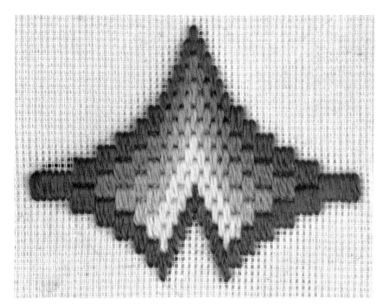

- Colorway #2: 510, Medium Green, 2 skeins; 527, Moss, 1 skein; 555, Green Giant, 1 skein; 570, Celery Leaf, 1 skein; 575, Spring Pea Green, 3 skeins.
- Colorway #3: 414, Rust, 2 skeins; 416, Light Rust, 1 skein; 423, Pale Rust, 1 skein; 425, Pink, 1 skein; 020, Natural, 3 skeins.

- One-half yard coordinating fabric for pillow back.

NOTE: Separate yarn and work with two-ply throughout.

STEP: Design is a 4-2 step.

INSTRUCTIONS: Tape canvas and mark for Four-way Bargello (see page 111).

Begin working at center of canvas, placing stitch "A," which is over six threads with the top touching the horizontal line. Carefully count the outline of several motifs. To avoid doing all the counting at once begin filling in and working white background as the counting progresses. Work out from the center to canvas edges.

Block and construct pillow (see page 117).

BARGELLO FLOWERS PILLOW

The soft freshness of pink and green brightened with white is an ever-popular color combination. The design is an easy repeat worked in the Four-way technique. The canvas is cream mono with seventeen threads to the inch. All elements combine to make a sixteen-inch pillow of quiet charm.

The basic floral motif of this pattern is a versatile design that can be used in many ways. It will be just as attractive worked in the traditional manner with or without the green zig-zag lines. The French Peasant Eyeglass Case on page 8 uses the floral as a simple repeat for a lovely fabric look. A dark background color changes the feeling of the overall design, again pointing out the many ways Bargello patterns can be modified.

510   555   570   281   865   005

FINISHED SIZE: 16″ x 16″.
MATERIALS:
- #17 cream mono canvas approximately 20″ x 20″.
- #22 tapestry needle.
- Persian yarn as follows: 510, Medium Green, 2 skeins; 555, Green Giant, 2 skeins; 570, Celery Leaf, 2 skeins; 281, Antique Pink, 2 skeins; 865, Powder Pink, 2 skeins; 005, White, 4 skeins.
- One-half yard appropriate fabric for pillow back.

NOTE: Separate yarn and work with two-ply throughout.
STEP: Design is a 4-2 step.

INSTRUCTIONS: Tape canvas and mark for Four-way Bargello as in chart on page 111.

Begin working in center of canvas by placing the four central flowers. Work out from center, following the chart.

Block and construct pillow following instructions on page 117.

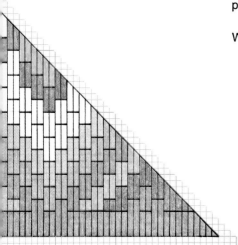

POMEGRANATE OCTAGON

The favorite old pomegranate pattern takes on a new look when it is worked Four-way in bright colors. The combination of five greened-down golds with three lively shades of the turquoise family has a decidedly modern flavor. The golds are adaptable to use with other accent colors also—true blues, greens, or reds would be attractive substitutes for the aquas. The pillow's interesting shape is an outgrowth of the pattern itself.

FINISHED SIZE: 14″ x 14″ at widest points.
MATERIALS:
  • #14 white mono canvas approximately 18″ x 18″.
  • #20 tapestry needle.
  • Persian yarn in the following assortment: 511, Pecan, 2 skeins; 521, Earth, 2 skeins; 531, Empire Gold, 2 skeins; 541, Gold, 2 skeins; 455, Light Gold, 2 skeins; 718, Blue Jade, 1 skein; 728, Light Aqua, 1 skein; 738, Medium Light Aqua, 1 skein.

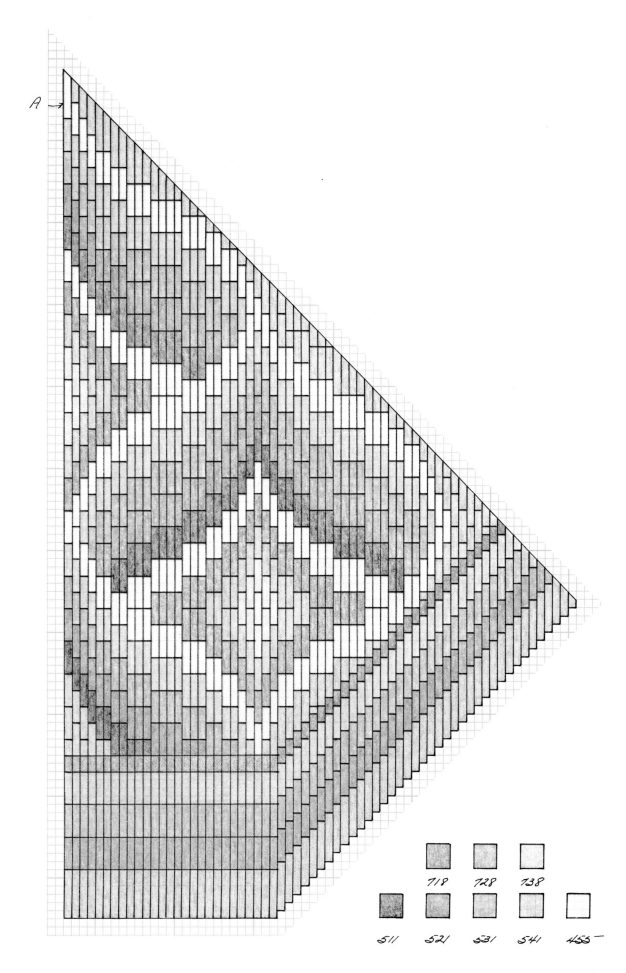

A →

718   728   738

511   521   531   541   455 ̄

35

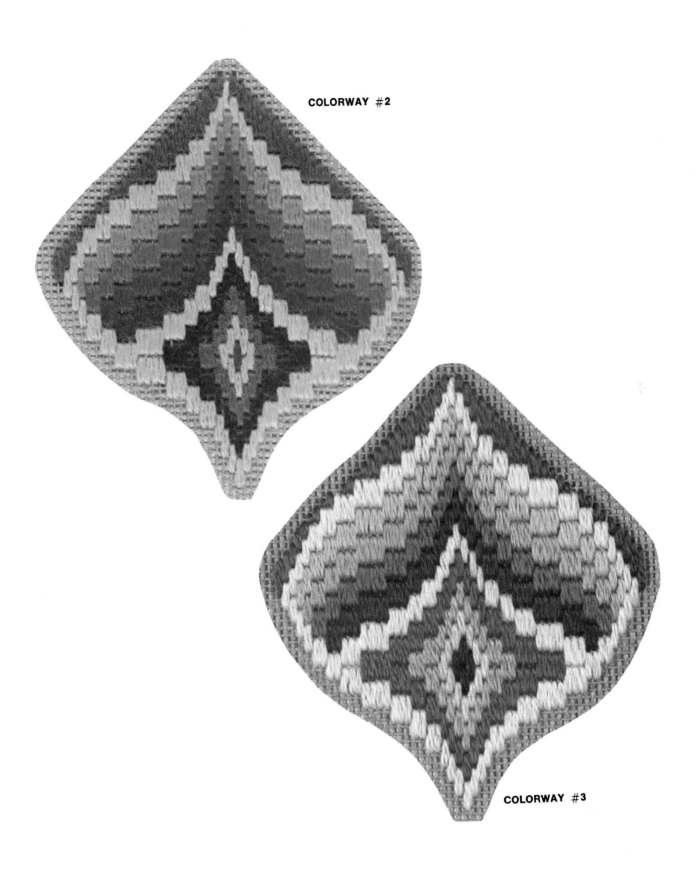

COLORWAY #2

COLORWAY #3

• Colorway #2: 217, Wood Brown, 2 skeins; 215, Cinnamon, 2 skeins; 414, Rust, 2 skeins; 416, Light Rust, 2 skeins; 454, Pale Pumpkin, 2 skeins; 520, Hunter Green, 1 skein; 510, Medium Green, 1 skein; 570, Celery Leaf, 1 skein.

• Colorway #3; 520, Hunter Green, 2 skeins; 510, Medium Green, 2 skeins; 555, Green Giant, 2 skeins; 570, Celery Leaf, 2 skeins; 575, Spring Pea Green, 2 skeins; 250, Tea Rose, 1 skein; 254, Dusty Pink, 1 skein; 831, Pale Pink, 1 skein.

• One-half yard coordinating fabric for pillow back.

NOTE: Separate yarn and work with two-ply throughout.

STEP: Design is a 4-2 step.

INSTRUCTIONS: Tape canvas and mark for Four-way Bargello (see page 111).

Start working with lightest gold by placing center stitch "A." Note that this stitch is over six threads. Stitches in balance of work are four threads long.

Plot all light-gold outlines on all four quadrants. Fill in motifs following the chart for color placement. Finish with Gobelin stitch borders in colors shown. Work a row of back stitch in matching color between rows of Gobelin stitches.

Block and construct pillow (see page 117).

RUST FOUR-WAY DIAMONDS

Interlocking diamonds in several sizes worked in a monochromatic scheme of shades of rust stand out in relief from a background of tent stitch. Combining the Bargello thus with the tent stitch serves to accent the Bargello and heighten its importance. Of course working the background in the small basket weave stitches is time consuming, and adds to the time usually needed to complete a Bargello project. If desired the background can be worked in brick stitch to speed the embroidery.

The interesting elongated effect in these diamonds is the result of combining stitches of both four- and six-thread lengths. Follow the chart carefully when establishing the pattern row.

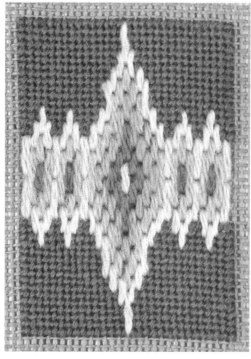

COLORWAY #2

COLORWAY #3

FINISHED SIZE: 13″ x 13″.
MATERIALS:
- #14 white mono canvas approximately 18″ x 18″.
- #20 tapestry needle.
- Persian yarn as follows: 414, Rust, 3 skeins; 416, Light Rust, 2 skeins; 426, Coral, 2 skeins; 436, Pale Coral, 2 skeins.

- Colorway #2; 510, Medium Green, 3 skeins; 555, Green Giant, 2 skeins; 570, Celery Leaf, 2 skeins; 575, Spring Pea Green, 2 skeins.

- Colorway #3; 740, Dark Blue, 3 skeins; 524, Dark Green, 2 skeins; R50, Dark Red, 2 skeins; 458, Daffodil, 2 skeins.

- One-half yard of coordinating fabric for pillow back.

NOTE: Separate yarn and work entire design with two-ply.
STEP: In this design the step is always up or down two threads, but the length of the stitches varies from four to six. Note also that some stitches used for filling in the motifs are eight threads long.

INSTRUCTIONS: Tape canvas and mark for Four-way Bargello (see page 111). Begin working at center with lightest shade yarn, placing stitch "A" at intersection of lines. Work all outlines of diamonds in all quadrants before filling in centers. If desired, work the tent stitch background a little at a time as the diamonds are worked out from the center.

Complete background of tent stitch for three rows beyond lower points of diamond pattern. Using the basket weave stitch for the background will help keep the piece in shape and make blocking simpler.

Block and construct pillow (see page 117). The pillow shown was finished with a crocheted braid inserted into the seam in lieu of the traditional piping. To make braid make a chain the length needed to reach around the pillow. Work two rows of single crochet. For this size pillow an extra skein of yarn was needed for the braid.

Center row - do not repeat.

414   416   426   436

40

FLORENTINE TILES PILLOW

This lovely pattern is the ultimate in Four-way design, for each motif is a separate mitered pattern. The individual flowerlike shapes are worked in Florentine stitch, shading from deep red at the center through soft roses to white at the edges. Two grays complete the design and form a secondary pattern where the motifs join. An interesting border pulls color and pattern together into an elegant pillow. Alternate color combinations of green and gold or blue and white offer variety but retain the delicate shadings that make this design so interesting.

This is a fairly intricate pattern, but one that is completely logical. It will require a little patience until the pattern is established, but then works easily.

COLORWAY #2   COLORWAY #3

FINISHED SIZE: 14″ x 14″.
MATERIALS:
- #13 tan mono canvas approximately 18″ x 18″.
- #20 tapestry needle.
- Persian yarn as follows: 236, Burgundy, 1 skein; 234, Toasty Pink, 1 skein; 281, Antique Pink, 2 skeins; 865, Powder Pink, 2 skeins; 182, Medium Slate Blue, 1 skein; 184, Silver Gray, 1 skein; 005, White, 1 skein.
- Colorway #2: 427, Medium Gold, 1 skein; 447, Mustard, 1 skein; 457, Canary Yellow, 2 skeins; 467, Light Medium Yellow, 2 skeins; 520, Hunter Green, 1 skein; 510, Medium Green, 1 skein.
- Colorway #3: 742, True Blue, 2 skeins; 752, Medium Blue, 2 skeins; 754, Light Medium Blue, 2 skeins; 756, Summer Blue, 2 skeins; 005, White, 1 skein.
- One-half yard coordinating fabric for pillow back.

NOTE: Separate yarn and work entire design with two-ply.
NOTE: This is a typical Florentine stitch, with stitches sewn over two and four threads. Reading up or down the rows, a long stitch is always followed by two short ones.

INSTRUCTIONS: Tape the canvas and mark for Four-way Bargello (see page 111). The diagonal lines on the canvas will correspond to line "A" on the chart. Although each individual motif is worked as a Four-way design, it is not necessary to draw all the miter lines. Use the lines on the canvas as a check to be certain that the motifs are placed correctly.

Begin by placing the four darkest stitches of the central motif directly on the dividing lines at the marked center of the canvas. (Since all motifs are exactly alike, it is easier to see the stitching pattern in one of the motifs shown in full rather than the quarter pattern at center of chart.)

Attach next shade and work around the center stitches, placing three stitches around each red stitch and then turning canvas one-quarter clockwise to place next group of three stitches. Continue working outward with color shading and following the chart for stitch length and placement until lightest shade has been used and "flower" motif is completed.

Working thus outward from the center has placed the design properly. From this point onward it will be best to work the lightest color outlining the motifs first, then work the shading in toward the centers. This will avoid counting mistakes, as all motifs join in a central mesh shared by the points of the petals.

Work all motifs in center field. Fill in arches at edges, following the chart. Work Gobelin stitch border.

Block and construct pillow (see page 117).

This design included courtesy the Columbia-Minerva Corp. A similar pillow on larger mesh canvas is available in kit form.

236   234   281   P65   182   184   005

FLORENTINE TILES EYEGLASS CASE

Miniature Four-way Florentine stitch designs in four shades of gold fit together tilelike to make an attractive eyeglass case large enough to accommodate fashionably big sunglasses. Green accents bring out the interesting flower-shaped motifs.

Each individual section is worked Four-way around four dark-green stitches that form its center. The design is less complicated than it appears, but does require an understanding of Four-way methods.
The curved top of the case, which was outlined with a row of tent stitch, was dictated by the natural shape of the design itself.

FINISHED SIZE: 3″ x 6¾″
MATERIALS:
- #12 mono canvas approximately 10″ x 11″.
- #20 tapestry needle.
- Persian yarn as follows: 427, Medium Gold, 1 skein; 447, Mustard, 1 skein; 441, Medium Yellow, 1 skein; 467, Light Yellow, 1 skein; 520, Hunter Green, 1 skein; 545, Avocado, 1 skein.
- Small piece of appropriate fabric for lining.

NOTE: The golds used in the floral-shaped designs are very adaptable and can be used with colors other than the greens shown as accents. Suggested changes would be blue, red, brown, rust, black with gray, or two shades of gray.

NOTE: Use yarn as it comes from the skein full-ply.

STEP: This is a typical Florentine stitch, with lengths varying over both two and four threads.

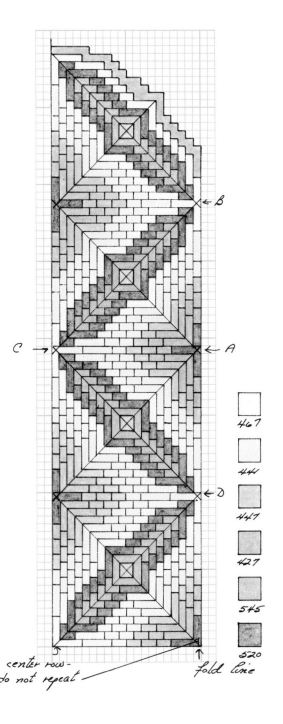

center row — do not repeat

fold line

467

444

447

427

545

520

INSTRUCTIONS: The chart shows half of either front or back of case. Tape canvas. Draw a line vertically down the center to indicate the fold line between front and back of case. Place center dark-green stitches forming cross "A" on fold line about 3½" from top of canvas. Lightly pencil in miter lines, radiating out from the cross about nine threads in each direction. Use these as a guide for first motif. They will not be needed for others.

Attach the darkest gold and work around the center stitches, placing three gold stitches around each green spoke, then turning the canvas one-quarter turn at the miter line to place the next group of three stitches until one row has been worked. Following the chart and using the established working method, work second row of darkest gold. Continue outward using colors in sequence shown, ending with lightest shade.

From this point on it will be best to work the lightest shade, outlining the motifs first to avoid counting errors. All motifs join in the central mesh shared by the points of the flower "petals" at "B," "C," and "D" on chart. Attach the palest gold at one of these points and count outline of the next motif. Continue until the shape is filled in with correct colors. When all motifs are worked, fill in the arches between with the greens as shown.

To make a neat edge at top of case, work a row of tent stitch along outline of design. This will make finishing without canvas showing possible.

Block completed Bargello and complete eyeglass case as in the instructions for French Peasant on page 10.

45

ROSEBUD PINCUSHION

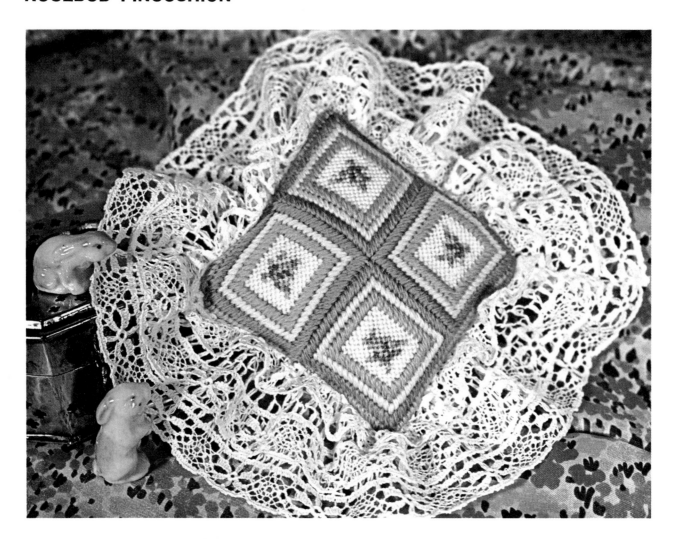

Petit point rosebuds in three shades of rose give this little pincushion
a dainty air. An additional part of its charm is derived from the square
shape, which is the result of working four diamonds in the Four-way
manner. Although the canvas is #17, quick-stitching Bargello fills most
of the area, leaving only the four one-inch squares to be filled in with petit
point. The result is a pretty dresser accessory.

Small items like this are welcome gifts, and are economical both
of time and materials. This one is a pleasant evening's occupation and
uses yarn left from a larger project.

FINISHED SIZE: 3½″ x 3½″.

MATERIALS:
- #17 cream mono canvas approximately 5″ x 5″.
- #22 tapestry needle.
- Persian yarn as follows: Project is so small that only a few yards of each color are required. Colors shown are 555, Green Giant; 570, Celery Leaf; 250, Tea Rose; 254, Dusty Pink; 831, Pale Pink; 005, White.

NOTE: Separate yarn and use two-ply for Bargello; one strand for petit point.

STEP: Bargello design is a 4-1 step.

INSTRUCTIONS: Tape canvas and mark for Four-way Bargello (see page 111). The chart shows one quadrant of the design from miter line to miter line. Begin with deepest shade of green at point "A" on the chart. Work outline of the diamond followed by the two rows inside. Work petit point rosebud, following the graph. Fill in background with white tent stitch. Work remaining three quadrants in the same manner. Add light-green border around outside edge.

Block and construct pincushion in manner similar to a pillow (see page 117). Add cording and tassels or finish extravagantly with wide cotton lace as in model.

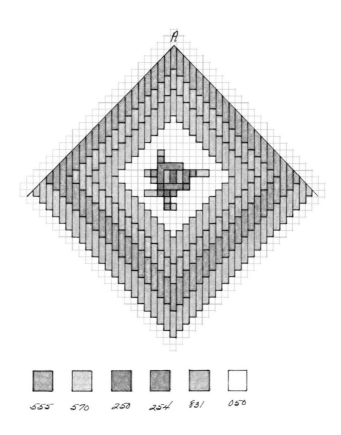

555   570   250   254   831   050

POMEGRANATE AND RIBBON PILLOW

Golden pomegranates and an undulating ribbon edge are silhoueted on a background of basket weave stitch on this unusual pillow. The flat background seems to emphasize the texture and color of the Bargello design as well as its outlines. The combination of golds and blues is elegant, a favorite of the author. However, the golds in the range shown are very versatile, and can be combined with other background colors if desired. Just as attractive as the blue would be dark green, red, wine, black, rust, or gray.

FINISHED SIZE: 14″ x 14″:
MATERIALS:
- #14 white mono canvas approximately 18″ x 18″.
- #20 tapestry needle.
- Persian yarn as follows: 405, Copper, 1 skein; 427, Medium Gold, 1 skein; 440, Topaz, 2 skeins; 457, Canary Yellow, 1 skein; 441,

Medium Yellow, 1 skein; 467, Light Medium Yellow, 1 skein; 763, Deep Teal, 5 skeins; 773, Teal, 1 skein; 783, Medium Teal, 1 skein; 756, Summer Blue, 1 skein.

Half-yard fabric in coordinating color for pillow back.

NOTE: Separate yarn and work with two-ply throughout.

INSTRUCTIONS: Tape canvas and mark for Four-way Bargello (see page 111). Beginning at "A" and counting stitches carefully from chart, work the outlines of the four pomegranates with color 440. Fill in motifs as shown in diagram.

Begin ribbon border at "B" with color 467 and work to miter lines on each side. Work succeeding rows as shown. Turn canvas and repeat for remaining three quadrants.

Work background preferably in basket weave stitch, but substitute continental if desired. Work only to miter lines of each quadrant, turning canvas just as to work the separate sections for Bargello. As soon as the Bargello is completed in one quadrant the background can be started and worked in small amounts rather than being left all to the last.

Work three rows of tent stitch in background color beyond the outer edge of the ribbon border.

Block and construct pillow (see page 117).

This design included courtesy The Columbia-Minerva Corp. A similar pillow on #12 canvas is available in kit form.

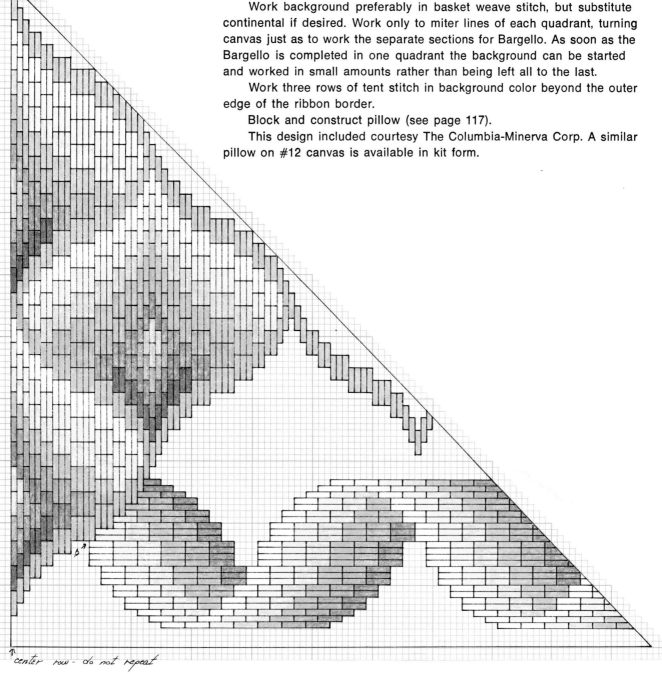

center row - do not repeat

405   427   440   457   441   467   763   773   783   756

49

KALEIDOSCOPE PANEL

COLORWAY #2

The kaleidoscope effect that comes so easily to Four-way Bargello is heightened in this design of overlapping diamonds. Further enhancement occurs because the diamonds are shaded light to dark, working out from the center.

Two colorways in full size illustrate the changes made in a design with radically different color treatment. The design is intricate and interesting in itself, and thus does not need a great deal of color variation. When worked in the monochromatic color scheme, the soft color gradings accentuate the design, according more importance to the design itself than to the color. On the other hand, the same design in shades of four brilliant colors allows the color to take over completely and literally earns the name Kaleidoscope. Managing this many colors—there are five shades of each—is a bit difficult, but if done carefully can result in a spectacular piece of Bargello.

On thirteen-mesh canvas these pieces are sixteen inches square, a size suitable to large pillows or panels. Fourteen-mesh canvas as a base will reduce them to fifteen inches, a more appropriate size for decorative cushions.

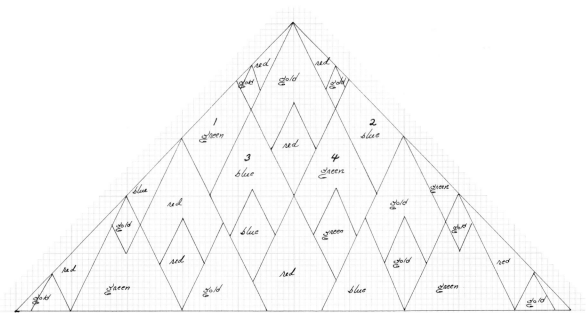

COLOR PLACEMENT FOR MULTICOLORED KALEIDOSCOPE

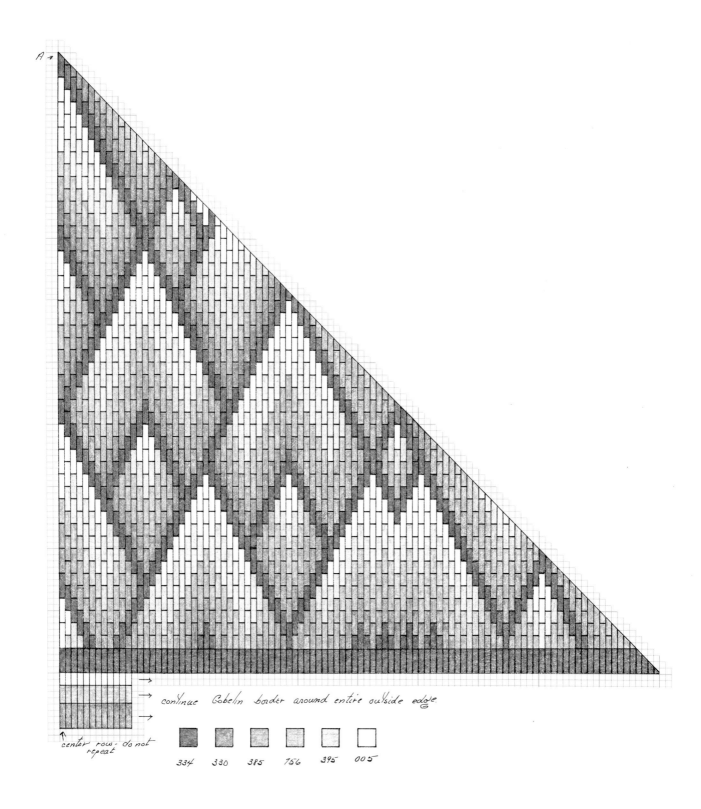

A →

continue Gobelin border around entire outside edge.

center row - do not repeat

334	330	385	756	395	005

MATERIALS:
- #13 tan mono canvas approximately 20" x 20".
- #20 tapestry needle.
- Persian yarn in the following assortment: 334, Dark French Blue, 3 skeins; 330, Old Blue, 2 skeins; 385, French Blue, 2 skeins; 756, Summer Blue, 1 skein; 395, Light Blue, 1 skein; 005, White, 2 skeins.

- Colorway #2—Kaleidoscope Multicolor: One skein each color:
    Greens: 504, Dark Green; 510, Medium Green; 555, Green Giant; 570, Celery Leaf; 575, Spring Pea Green.
    Blues: 740, Dark Blue; 742, True Blue; 743, Medium True Blue; 781, Light True Blue.
    Golds: 427, Medium Gold; 447, Mustard; 441, Medium Yellow; 442, Yellow; 456, Baby Yellow.
    Reds: 810, Deep Red; R10, True Red; 958, Dark Orange; 970, Light Orange; 456, Baby Yellow.
    Brown: 113

- One-half yard fabric for back of pillow or framing materials as shown.

NOTE: Separate yarn and work with two-ply throughout.

STEP: Entire design is a 4-2 step.

INSTRUCTIONS: Tape canvas and mark for Four-way Bargello (see page 111). Start working at center of canvas with a stitch over six threads—"A" on chart. Plot dark-blue diamond outlines on entire quadrant. Beginning with center diamond, fill in the motifs, shading the color out from center as shown on the chart.

Work all four sections in this manner. Finish with Gobelin border as shown. Between rows of Gobelin stitches work a row of back stitches with a single strand of yarn in matching color.

Work multicolored design as above, but follow small chart for color placement of individual diamonds. Shading is handled in exactly same manner as for blue version. Work one quadrant as noted on the small chart. Turn canvas and work second quadrant, making the following changes in color distribution: Allow diamonds 1 and 2 to continue into the next section, matching the one already worked. Then to avoid having two neighboring diamonds in the same color, reverse the colors in diamonds 3 and 4. Work the Gobelin border for this version as for the blue, but work one row brown, one row darkest gold, one darkest blue, and one of the darkest green.

Block and finish as desired (see page 115).

PASTEL PARFAIT PILLOW I

This pillow is an ideal introduction to the art of combining patterns into a pleasing composition. Two very easy patterns—the scallop and a small diamond—are worked in bright pastels on #14 white mono canvas. An added Gobelin stitch border between the designs and outlining the outside edge helps tie the designs together.

FINISHED SIZE: 12″ x 12″.
MATERIALS:
- #14 white mono canvas approximately 16″ x 16″.
- #20 tapestry needle.
- Persian yarn as follows: 853, Flesh, 1 skein; 458, Daffodil, 1 skein; G74, Light Apple Green, 1 skein; 756, Summer Blue, 1 skein; 005, White, 3 skeins; 641, Light Mauve, 1 skein.
- Colorway #2: 958, Dark Orange, 1 skein; 970, Light Orange, 1 skein; 545, Avocado, 1 skein; 492, Dust, 1 skein; 405, Copper, 3 skeins.
- One-half yard appropriate fabric for pillow back.

NOTE: Additional color combinations applicable to this pillow are shown with Pastel Parfait Pillows II and III (pages 58 and 62).

NOTE: Separate yarn and work with two-ply. If desired work a row of back stitches between Gobelin rows of borders, using a single strand of yarn.

STEP: Both patterns in the pillow are 4-2 step.

INSTRUCTIONS: Tape canvas (see page 110) and mark as shown in Chart #1 (page 111) with the four lines "A," "B," "C," and "D." Draw the lines carefully as noted in the text.

     The pillow is worked in two sections beginning with the center square in the scallop design. In the square, rows are worked across as in traditional Bargello. Borders in the small diamond design are worked as in Four-way Bargello.

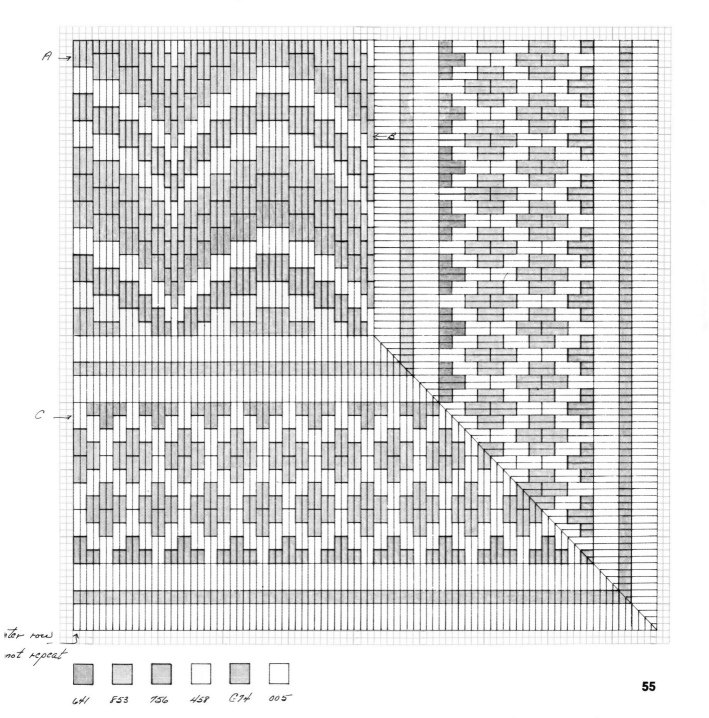

641   853   756   458   674   005

COLORWAY #2

With color 641 (Light Mauve) begin working at center of canvas with stitch "A." Carefully count and work across to "B." End yarn. Attach again at "A" and work remaining half of row to left edge of square, reading chart again from "A" to "B" but stitching from right to left. Continue working downward to complete half of center section as diagramed. Turn canvas. Keeping the color sequence as established, fill in remaining ten rows to finish square (last row will be blue).

Work white Gobelin stitch border around entire square, mitering corners as shown on chart on page 107. Count stitches carefully to be certain that the number corresponds to chart.

Finish second and third rows of border. Corners of Gobelin rows should be on miter lines "C" and "D."

Begin diamond border at "C." Work across to miter line and check to be certain that pattern works out as charted. Plot all white diamonds in the section. Fill in centers in colors shown. Work three other sections in the same manner. Do not be confused by the fact that this pillow has only a vertical center row. If chart is followed, design will be perfect.

Work outside Gobelin border on all four sides. Using a single strand of matching thread, work a row of back stitches between rows of Gobelin.

Block and construct pillow, following instruction on page 117.

PASTEL PARFAIT PILLOW II

A pretty pastel confection, this pillow combines Bargello, tent stitch, and touches of embroidery. The colors are the same as those of its mates on pages 54 and 60, pointing out the desirability of making several pillows in a single color combination but varying designs so that they can be used as a grouping.

FINISHED SIZE: 13″ x 13″.
MATERIALS:
- #14 white mono canvas approximately 17″ x 17″.
- #20 tapestry needle.
- Persian yarn as follows: 853, Flesh, 1 skein; 458, Daffodil, 1 skein; G74, Light Apple Green, 1 skein; 756, Summer Blue, 1 skein; 641, Light Mauve, 1 skein; 005, White, 3 skeins.

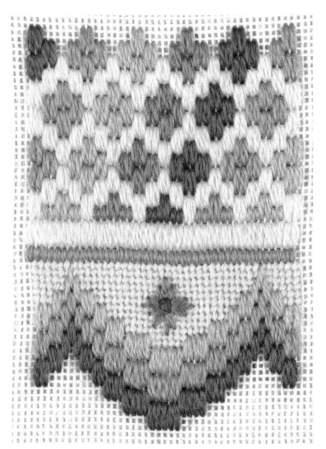

**PASTEL PARFAIT PILLOW II AND III—
DETAIL OF EMBROIDERY**

COLORWAY #2

• Colorway #2: 510, Medium Green, 1 skein; 555, Green Giant, 1 skein; 570, Celery Leaf, 1 skein; 281, Antique Pink, 1 skein; 575, Spring Pea Green, 3 skeins.

• One-half yard appropriate fabric for pillow back.

NOTE: Additional color combinations applicable to this pillow are shown with Pastel Parfait Pillows I and III on pages 54 and 62.

NOTE: Separate yarn and work with two-ply throughout, including embroidery stitches and portion worked in tent stitch.

NOTE: The embroidery stitches in the border are worked on top of the tent stitches.

STEP: Both patterns in the pillow are 4-2 step.

INSTRUCTIONS: Tape canvas and mark for Four-way Bargello (see page 111).

The pillow is worked in two sections, beginning with the center square, which is a small diamond design. In this center panel the Bargello is worked in the traditional manner, with rows running straight across the canvas. In the border sections the pattern is worked as for Four-way Bargello.

To center the design and avoid a counting error, first work a yellow diamond, placing stitch "A" on the center vertical with the top of the stitch touching the horizontal line. Now begin working the white outlines, beginning under the diamond at "B." Plot all of the white in center panel before beginning to fill in colors. The completed center square contains thirteen rows of white.

Outline square with Gobelin stitch border. Miter the corners as shown on page 107. Count the number of stitches in Gobelin outline and compare to chart to insure accuracy.

Work the three-row scallop design in the border. Fill in the spaces with tent stitch. Add Gobelin border. Work embroidery on top of tent stitches placing as shown (see detail photograph). Flowers are long stitches with French knot centers.

Using a single strand of yarn in a matching color, work a row of back stitches between rows of Gobelin in borders.

Block and construct pillow (see page 117).

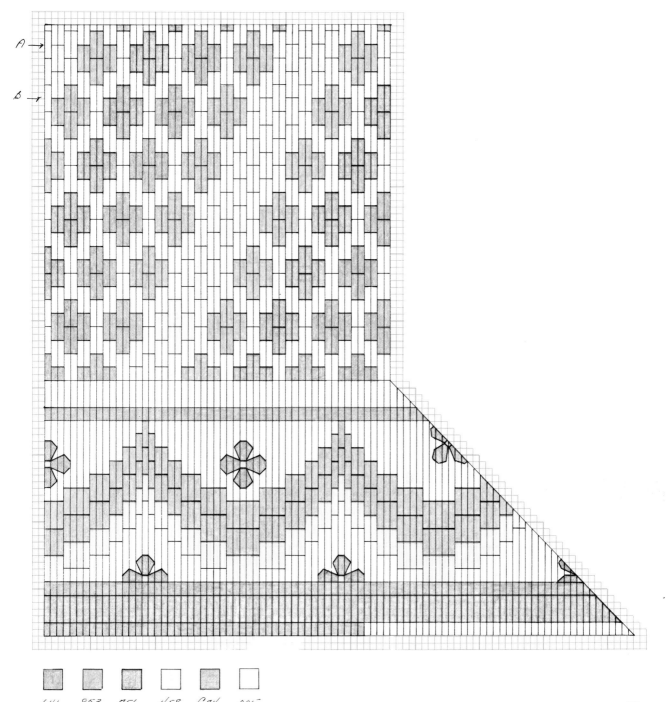

641   853   756   458   C74   005

PASTEL PARFAIT PILLOW III

Three Bargello designs in pastel colors combine with a variety of stitches in a pillow that is interesting to work and looks far more complicated than it really is. Actually the three Bargello patterns are easy ones to work—it is their combination plus the mitered corner borders that produce the intriguing detail.

For the center panel a small diamond repeat is carried out in six colors. Texture and interest are added by working the smallest diamonds in the diamond eyelet stitch. A narrow Gobelin border sets the panel apart from the border surrounding it. In the wider of the frames a single row of each of the pastel shades forms the scallop pattern, which seems to be raised above the white tent stitch background. Tiny pink flowers with French knot centers adorn the white needlepoint.

Following another narrow Gobelin border is an easy row of small diamonds in blue, yellow, and white. A final Gobelin stitch margin is green and mauve. All elements add to a third coordinating pillow for the pastel group.

center row - do not repeat

641   853   752   458   G74   005

COLORWAY #2

FINISHED SIZE: 14″ x 14″.

MATERIALS:
- #14 white mono canvas approximately 18″ x 18″.
- #20 tapestry needle.
- Persian yarn as follows: 853, Flesh, 1 skein; 458, Daffodil, 1 skein; G74, Light Apple Green, 1 skein; 756, Summer Blue, 1 skein; 641, Light Mauve, 1 skein; 005, White, 3 skeins.

- Colorway #2: R10, True Red, 1 skein; 458, Daffodil, 1 skein; 559, Brilliant Green, 1 skein; 742, True Blue, 1 skein; 611, Gypsy Blue, 1 skein; 005, White, 3 skeins.

- One-half yard appropriate fabric for pillow back.

NOTE: Additional colorways applicable to this pillow are shown with Pastel Parfait Pillows I and II on pages 54 and 58.

NOTE: Separate yarn and work with two-ply throughout, including embroidery stitches and tent stitch.

NOTE: The embroidery stitches in the scallop border are worked on top of the tent stitches.

STEP: Diamond pattern in center square is a 4-1 step. Scallop and diamond designs in borders are both 4-2 step.

INSTRUCTIONS: Tape canvas and mark for Four-way Bargello (see page 111).

Work the pillow in three sections, completing each before starting next.

Begin with the center square, placing the pink diamond eyelet stitch over the intersection of the dividing lines on the canvas. The four long stitches that form the axis of the eyelet are over six threads each. If these are placed first, followed by the yellow diamond, much counting will be avoided. Following the chart out from this point, finish the square as shown.

Outline the panel with the Gobelin border in blue and yellow. Check alignment with the miter lines on the canvas. Corners should be on the miter lines.

Start scallop pattern at center of chart and work five rows as shown. Fill in spaces with tent stitch in white. Add Gobelin border and embroidery stitches on top of the needlepoint. (See detail of embroidery on page 58.)

Work third and final pattern, beginning again at center of chart. Finish with Gobelin border in mauve and green. Place a row of back stitches between rows of Gobelin stitches to cover any white canvas that might show.

Block and construct pillow (see page 117).

WOVEN COVERLET PILLOW

Elsa Williams tapestry yarn on eighteen-mesh canvas results in a satiny smooth piece of Bargello with a texture and design akin to those of the antique woven coverlets of this country. The simple coloring of dusty blue and white heightens the similarity, but the design will be equally effective in many two-color combinations.

As worked on the fine canvas the pillow measures 11½″ x 11½″. Translating to larger canvas will produce a larger pillow and perhaps make the design more appealing to those who have not yet experimented with the fine canvases. For instance, fourteen-mesh canvas and Persian yarn could be used for a pillow roughly 15″ x 15″.

A →

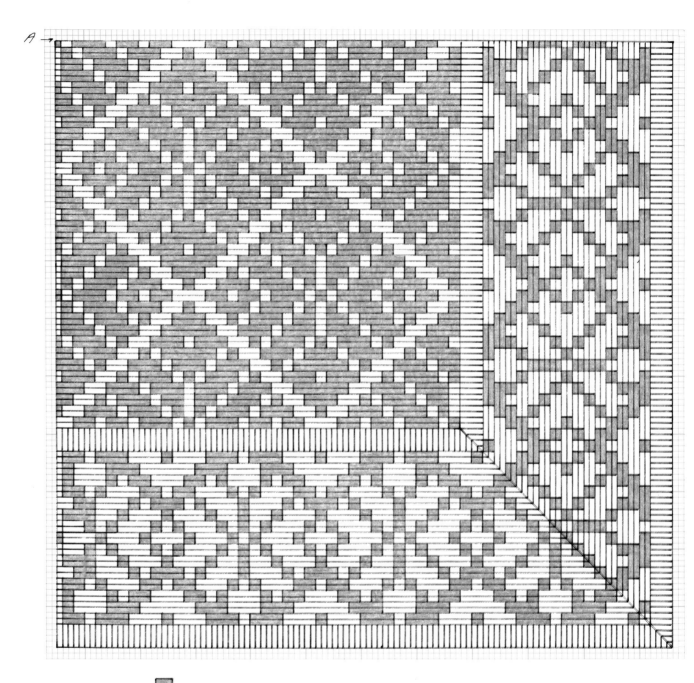

505

805

FINISHED SIZE: 11½″ x 11½″.
MATERIALS:
- #18 white mono canvas approximately 15″ x 15″.
- #22 tapestry needle.
- Elsa Williams tapestry yarn as follows: 505, Blue, 3 skeins; 805, White, 2 skeins.
- One-half yard appropriate fabric for pillow back.

NOTE: Use yarn just as it comes from the skein, full-ply.

NOTE: The field of the pillow and upper and lower portions of the borders are worked horizontally—the side borders with the stitches vertical as usual. The step is not regular as the stitches are sewn over two, four, six, eight, and ten threads.

INSTRUCTIONS: Tape canvas and mark horizontal and vertical lines through center. Miter lines will be needed for border but can be added after Gobelin border outlining center has been worked.

Begin working at center of canvas, placing stitch "A" just under the horizontal line. This stitch is over two threads; the chart shows only half of the center portion of the motif. Since all motifs are alike it is easier to work the first one following one of those that are shown in total. (A) indicates relative position of "A" on complete motif.

The design is a regular repeat that is easiest worked one color at a time. Work all of center panel; outline with white Gobelin border; finish with outside frame. When counting this border note the slight variation in design in center of top and bottom to compensate for the fact that center panel is not exactly square. Finish with Gobelin border.

Block and construct pillow (see page 117).

PORTUGUESE FLORAL PILLOW

Needlepoint designs are found in many unexpected places. The floral center of an old Portugese earthenware plate was the inspiration for a small panel in the lovely colors found so often in that country. Combining the tent stitch square with a wide border of Bargello in the same colors seemed a natural thing. The result is a very unusual pillow.

FINISHED SIZE: 14½″ x 14½″.
MATERIALS:
- #14 white mono canvas approximately 18″ x 18″.
- #20 tapestry needle.
- Persian yarn as follows: 740, Dark Blue, 3 skeins; 240, Cranberry, 2 skeins; 545, Avocado, 2 skeins; 440, Topaz, 2 skeins; 005, White, 2 skeins.

- Colorway #2: 405, Copper, 3 skeins; 210, Henna, 2 skeins; 545, Avocado, 2 skeins; 445, Antique Gold, 2 skeins; 020, Natural, 2 skeins

- One-half yard coordinating fabric for pillow back.

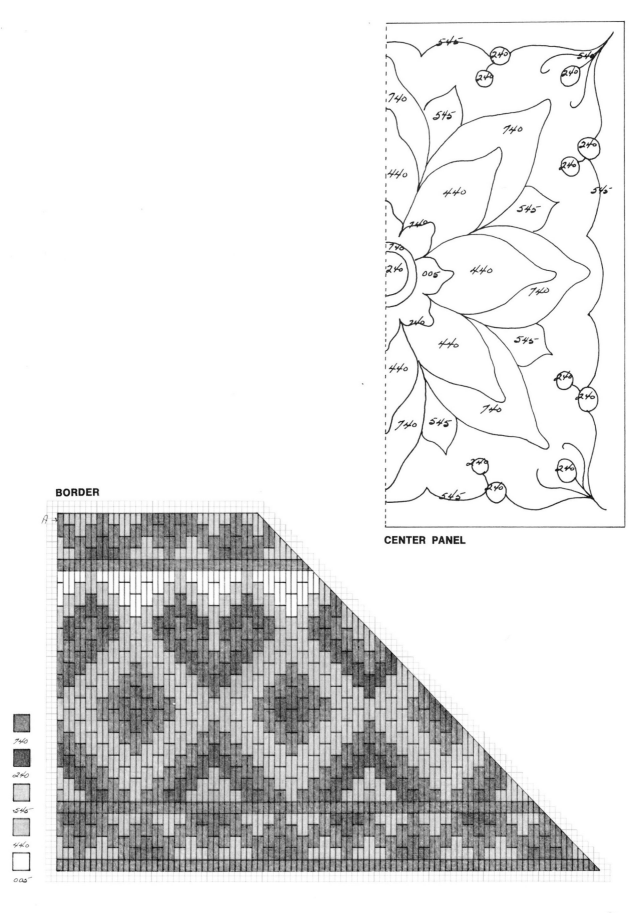

CENTER PANEL

BORDER

67

NOTE: Separate yarn and work with two-ply throughout.

INSTRUCTIONS: Tape canvas and mark for Four-way Bargello (see page 111). Fold a piece of tracing paper in half vertically. Lay fold line over the dotted line on the drawing of the center panel. Trace. Turn tracing paper over and trace the image to other side of the paper. Open flat. Lay the marked canvas over tracing with center of canvas over center of flower and with vertical line matching fold line of paper. Trace the flower and vine onto the canvas.

Work the center panel in tent stitch—preferably the basket weave. Finished panel should be exactly seventy-one stitches square. Work one additional row of tent stitch around the panel in dark blue.

Begin the Bargello border at center of edge of panel, at "A" on the chart. Work as shown, following the chart for color placement. Work a row of back stitch in blue between the rows of plain Gobelin stitches.

Block and construct the pillow (see page 117).

COLORWAY #2

FLORENTINE GARDEN PILLOW

The colors in this little pillow are the lovely pastels often considered early American—soft shades of French blue, dusty pinks, and greens in three easy tints. The center rectangle is worked in an old Florentine scallop design, while the border of stylized flowers repeats identical colors. Gobelin borders and fat tassels are trim finishing touches.

FINISHED SIZE: 9″ x 12″.
MATERIALS:
- #14 white mono canvas approximately 13″ x 16″.
- #20 tapestry needle.
- Persian yarn as follows: 510, Medium Green, 1 skein; 570, Celery Leaf, 1 skein; 575, Spring Pea Green, 1 skein; 255, Rose, 1 skein; 865, Powder Pink, 1 skein; 385, French Blue, 1 skein; 395, Light Blue, 1 skein; 012, Ivory, 1 skein.
- One-half yard fabric in coordinating color for pillow back.
- Tassels require 1 extra skein of 510, Medium Green.

NOTE: Separate yarn and work with two-ply throughout.

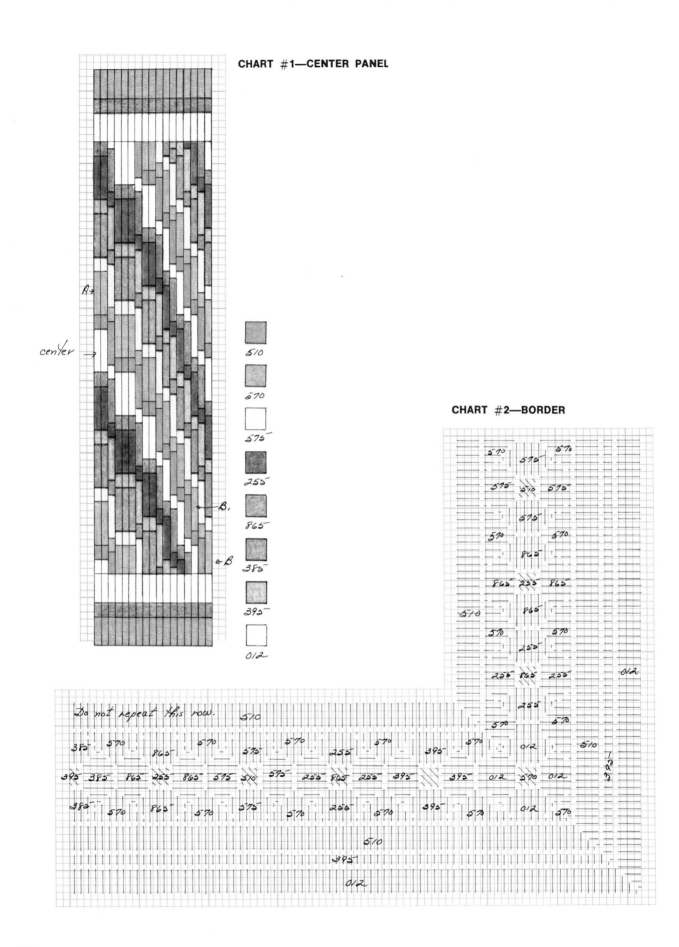

CHART #1—CENTER PANEL

CHART #2—BORDER

INSTRUCTIONS: The fact that both types of chart are used for this pillow does not indicate that it is difficult to work, but that the change in the direction of the stitching of the border could not be shown properly on the color chart. Since the reader is accustomed to the easy-to-read color diagrams, it was decided to use it for the center panel and place only the border on the black-and-white chart for accuracy. Explicit instructions for combining the two follow in the directions below.

Tape the canvas and mark for traditional Bargello (see page 111). The color chart shows one-half of the center scallop pattern. Begin with color 570 (Celery Leaf) at "A," placing this stitch next to the vertical line with the bottom of the stitch six mesh above the horizontal line. Following the chart, work from "A" to "B." Continuing to work to right edge while reading the chart from "B" to "A" and back again, establish a line of 1½ scallops. (Do not repeat stitches at "A" and "B.") Attach yarn again at center stitch and complete row to left edge of rectangle. There is now a line of three large scallops on the canvas, and all succeeding rows may be worked all the way across the panel. Continuing to follow the chart for correct color sequence, work the entire rectangular panel. Finish the panel with three Gobelin borders, as shown.

Draw miter lines extending out from the corners of the rectangle. Move to the black-and-white chart. The lines indicate the actual threads of the canvas. If an ink line crosses four of the grid lines it indicates that the stitch is to be taken over four canvas threads. To help orient this chart to the already completed work, the last green Gobelin border of the rectangle has been shown. *Do not repeat this row!*

Begin working the floral border at the center and work to the miter line at the right edge. Return to the center and repeat the pattern to the left, reading the chart from left to right. This is to keep the color sequence correct.

Attach ivory yarn and complete corner flower on right miter line. Work to center of side border, placing colors as indicated. The last flower shown on the chart is palest green, color 575. Continue working flower motifs to top corner, but use colors 385, 395, and 255 in that order for the next three flowers. End at miter line with a flower in ivory to match the one at lower corner. Work the remaining two borders to match their counterparts. Finish with three rows of Gobelin stitch for a border as shown. With a single strand of yarn in matching color work a row of back stitches between Gobelin rows.

Block and construct pillow (see page 117). Directions for making tassels are on page 118.

FLORENTINE SCALLOP PILLOW

This beautiful pillow was made using only the scallop design forming the center panel of the Florentine Garden Pillow (page 69) to illustrate the versatility of the designs. The pastel colors were only slightly altered, but the canvas size was increased to ten mesh. Since the pattern adapts so well to an oblong-shaped piece, that was retained. This is an easy pillow to make and is a good introduction to the method of working the Florentine stitches.

FINISHED SIZE: 14″ x 10″.

MATERIALS:
- #10 white interlocking canvas approximately 18″ x 14″.
- #18 tapestry needle.
- Persian yarn as follows: 843, Fireball, 2 skeins; 853, Flesh, 2 skeins; 555, Green Giant, 2 skeins; 575, Spring Pea Green, 2 skeins; 385, French Blue, 2 skeins; 395, Light Blue, 2 skeins.
- One-half yard coordinating fabric for pillow back.

NOTE: If pillow is to be finished with tassels as shown, an additional skein of 385, French Blue, will be required. Make tassels following the instructions included with directions for finishing pillows on page 118.

NOTE: Use yarn full-ply throughout. If yarn does not cover adequately add an extra strand.

STEP: This is a typical Florentine step, with stitches over both six and two threads. The key to the design is that a short stitch is always placed directly beneath a long one, and vice versa.

INSTRUCTIONS: Tape canvas and mark for traditional Bargello (see page 111). Using chart on page 70, with color 575 (palest green) in the needle, begin working at "A" on the chart, and placing the stitch on center lines, work as far as "B-1" on chart. Continuing to stitch to right, but counting back up to "A" work half of the next scallop. Repeat to complete 2½ arches. End yarn and attach again at center at "A." Work to left to complete five scallops. All subsequent rows can be worked all the way across the canvas.

Use colors in the following order, working downward: 575 (first row already counted); 555, 853, 853, 385, and 395. Next row of 575 is the last full row, reaching the lower edge of the piece. Continue color sequence as established to square off edge. Turn canvas and work to complete keeping color order. Eleven full rows ending with deep green will reach upper edge. Fill in remaining spaces as for lower edge.

Block and construct pillow (see page 117).

DOUBLE BORDERED DIAMONDS PILLOW

In this little pillow three related diamond patterns are combined in shades of rust and blue. Each design is basically a diamond, and each is easy to work. Some of the centers are worked in the diamond eyelet stitch to add texture, and French knots in the outer border add extra fillip. Plain Gobelin rows between the patterns define each but at the same time tie all elements into a pleasing composition.

Colorway #2 retains the four rust shades and substitutes greens for the blues; a minor adjustment, but one that points out the ease with which a color change can be made to fit individual needs.

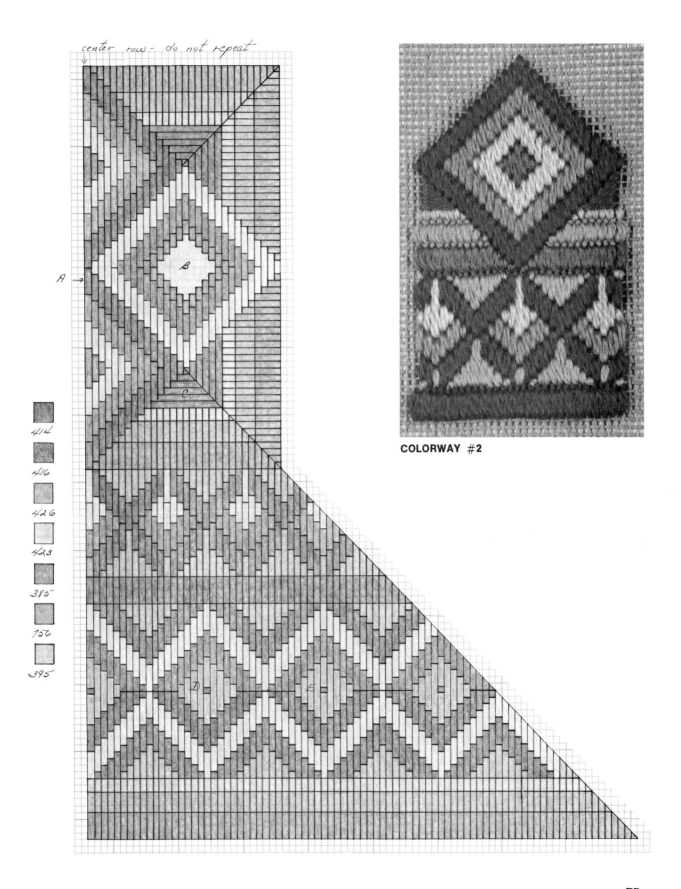

center row - do not repeat

A →

B

C

D   E

414

416

426

423

385

156

395

COLORWAY #2

FINISHED SIZE: 12″ x 12″.

MATERIALS:
- #14 white mono canvas.
- #20 tapestry needle.
- Persian yarn as follows: 414, Rust, 1 skein; 416, Light Rust, 1 skein; 426, Indian Pink, 1 skein; 423, Pale Rust, 1 skein; 385, French Blue, 1 skein; 756, Summer Blue, 1 skein; 395, Light Blue, 1 skein.

- Colorway #2: 414, Rust, 1 skein; 416, Light Rust, 1 skein; 426, Indian Pink, 1 skein; 423, Pale Rust, 1 skein; 510, Medium Green, 1 skein; 555, Green Giant, 1 skein; 570, Celery Leaf, 1 skein.

- One-half yard coordinating fabric for pillow back.

NOTE: Separate yarn and work with two-ply throughout.

STEP: Entire design is a 4-1 step.

INSTRUCTIONS: Tape canvas and mark as for Four-way Bargello (see page 111). The chart shows one-half of the center square—one-eighth of border.

Place stitch "A" on canvas directly over center vertical line, with top touching the horizontal. This will center design correctly. Work the four diamonds following the chart. Center "B" is to be worked in the diamond eyelet stitch.

Next, finish the Gobelin border around the diamonds. Fill in corners "C" with long stitches mitering along line as shown. Continue working to outside edge to complete borders. Centers of diamonds in outer frame are to be worked again in diamond eyelit stitch—"D." French knots—"E" —fill opening in middle of eyelet filling.

With one strand of yarn in matching colors work a row of back stitch between rows of Gobelin stitch. Block and construct pillow (see page 117).

VIBRANT PANEL

The concept of using Bargello framed as a picture or wall hanging
has been virtually overlooked, but some compositions are too handsome
to be used any other way. This vibrant panel is a good case in point.
Three different designs combine in a careful blend with seven bright
colors. The outer border, an updated version of the favorite old fish-scale
design, uses all seven colors, working from yellow to orange to red,
then from yellow through the greens to dark blue. A small floral border
using red, yellow, and two of the darker greens is outlined in blue.
The center panel is a small Four-way design using all seven colors
again, but in an entirely different manner. The secret ingredient tying
all three patterns into a whole is the careful use of color arrangement.

The alternate colorway, using soft shades of rust and green, will work up as a more subdued but equally attractive piece.

After extolling the piece's beauty as a wall panel, it must be observed that it would also make a lovely pillow. As worked on thirteen-mesh canvas the piece measures 15 inches square. If the canvas size were to be changed to #14, the resulting needlepoint would measure approximately 14″ x 14″, the traditional size for pillow tops.

FINISHED SIZE: 15″ x 15″.
MATERIALS:

- #13 mesh tan canvas approximately 19″ x 19″.
- #20 tapestry needle.
- Persian yarn as follows: 559, Brilliant Green, 2 skeins; 569, Apple Green, 2 skeins; 579, Light Green, 1 skein; 458, Daffodil, 1 skein; 718, Blue Jade, 2 skeins; 978, Medium Orange, 1 skein; 958, Dark Orange, 1 skein.

- Colorway #2: 414, Rust, 2 skeins; 416, Light Rust, 2 skeins; 423, Pale Rust, 1 skein; 454, Pale Pumpkin, 1 skein; 528, Forest Green, 2 skeins; 570, Celery Leaf, 1 skein; 555, Green Giant, 1 skein; 575, Spring Pea Green, 1 skein.

NOTE: Separate yarn and work with two-ply throughout.

STEP: Design is basically a 4-2 step except for portions of the inner border that are not worked as true Bargello, but rather in the manner of embroidery. Note also the variance in stitch length along curve of fish-scale motifs to make pattern fit within the curve.

INSTRUCTIONS: Tape canvas and mark for Four-way Bargello (see page 111). Work in three sections. Begin with center square; add narrow border; finish with wider fish-scale frame.

With red yarn (958) work small floral motif that forms apex of center design. Work so that long stitches "A" intersect where lines on canvas cross. Next establish blue outlines. Fill in motifs following chart for color placement. Add blue Gobelin stitch border.

Begin narrow floral border with the red at center of chart. Work all flowers. Fill in centers with Smyrna cross in yellow. Add background of greens and blue Gobelin border.

Fish-scale border should also be started at center and all blue outlines established before filling in motifs. Note changes in stitch length in most colors along edge of motifs.

Add the three Gobelin stitch borders in colors shown. With a single strand of yarn in matching shade, work a row of back stitch between rows of Gobelin.

Block and frame or construct as a pillow (see page 117).

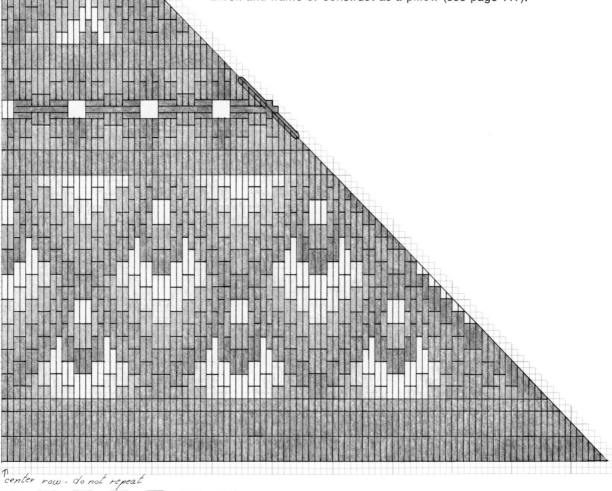

↑ center row - do not repeat

559   569   579   718   958   978   458

MOORISH PANEL

Most designs are adaptable to uses other than the one shown in this book. The Moorish Panel would make a handsome pillow as well as the attractive wall hanging that shows off its intricate border to such good advantage. The simple unadorned metal frame is a perfect complement to the bright colors and interesting stitch patterns. Many of the other pieces will be just as lovely framed as they are in the finished form illustrated.

The tent stitch square, an adaptation of the ethnic designs found in many areas, establishes the color scheme for the entire piece. The wide border is primarily a Florentine Wave design, with the open areas filled in with tiny diamonds of upright Gobelin stitch. This is not an especially difficult pattern, but it is one that requires patience.

COLORWAY #2

FINISHED SIZE: 14½″ x 14½″.
MATERIALS:

- #13 tan mono canvas approximately 18″ x 18″.
- #20 tapestry needle.
- Persian yarn as follows: 005, Black, 2 skeins; 752, Medium Blue, 3 skeins; R60, Medium Dark Red, 2 skeins; G74, Light Apple Green, 2 skeins; 458, Daffodil, 2 skeins.

- Colorway #2: 182, Medium Slate Blue, 2 skeins; 184, Silver Gray, 3 skeins; 005, White, 2 skeins; 186, Silver Blue, 2 skeins; R10, True Red, 2 skeins.

- Colorway #3: 217, Wood Brown, 2 skeins; 718, Blue Jade, 3 skeins; 545, Avocado, 2 skeins; 843, Fireball, 2 skeins; 447, Mustard, 2 skeins.

- Framing materials if square is to be used as a picture, as shown. One-half yard coordinating fabric if piece is to be finished as a pillow.

NOTE: Separate yarn and work with two-ply throughout.
STEP: The Florentine Wave pattern in the border is a 6-1 step. Small diamonds are worked over two, four, and six threads in a one-step progression, as shown on the chart.

INSTRUCTIONS: Tape canvas and mark for Four-way Bargello (see page 111). Work the tent stitch square first, placing the red stitch "A" over the intersection of the dividing lines. After the red center stitches are worked it will be easiest to work all black outlines, leaving large blocks of color to be filled in later. Outline completed square with Gobelin border. Check to make certain that corners of borders are on miter lines.

Begin Florentine Wave design at center of panel ("B" on chart). Complete yellow rows on all four sides of piece. Then work back toward the middle, filling in the black Florentine row and the diamonds. Next finish working to outside of border. Add Gobelin row at edge to complete design.

Block and finish as desired (see page 115).

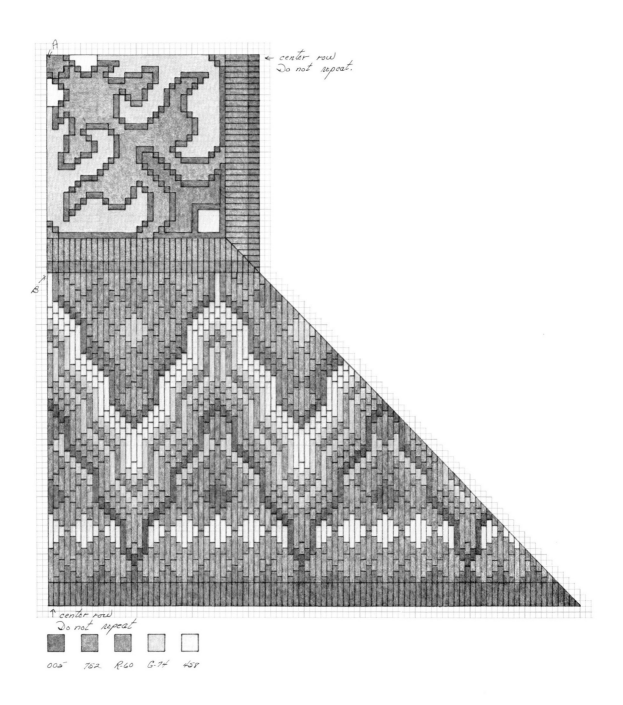

← center row
Do not repeat.

↑ center row
Do not repeat

005   752   R-60   G-74   458

83

INTERLOCKING SQUARES

Geometric design, which speaks to a human need for order, has always been favored. That is part of the reason for Bargello's enduring appeal; versatility is another. Both that versatility and the symmetry of an ordered geometric are found in this panel of rust highlighted with blue.

The two interlocking squares frame an easy Four-way square worked in soft shades of rust. A pattern of tiny shaded diamonds is an unobtrusive inner border, changing color where it is overlapped by the blue square. A motif from the center section is modified and becomes the pattern for the outside border. Wide Gobelin bands repeat the rust square, tying the various patterns together.

COLORWAY #2

COLORWAY #3

85

414   763

416   783

423   765

425

None of the designs used is particularly advanced, but the combination gives the appearance of a very difficult piece. These designs do require a great deal of patience on the part of the designer, but the reader is spared that. It is hoped that many will be encouraged to try original compositions after working several of these.

FINISHED SIZE: 14½″ x 14½″.
MATERIALS:
- #14 white mono canvas approximately 18″ x 18″.
- #20 tapestry needle.
- Persian yarn as follows: 414, Rust, 2 skeins; 416, Medium Rust, 2 skeins; 423, Light Rust, 1 skein; 425, Indian Pink, 1 skein; 763, Deep Teal, 1 skein; 783, Medium Teal, 1 skein; 765, Light Teal, 1 skein.

- Colorway #2: Rust shades same as above. Substitute greens for blues as follows: 520, Hunter, 1 skein; 555, Green Giant, 1 skein; 570, Celery Leaf, 1 skein.

- Colorway #3: 521, Earth, 2 skeins; 531, Empire Gold, 3 skeins (use for both middle rusts); 467, Light Gold, 1 skein; 718, Teal, 1 skein; 728, Light Aqua, 1 skein; 748, Turquoise, 1 skein.

NOTE: Separate yarn and work with two-ply throughout.
STEP: Both a 4-2 and a 4-1 step are used. This will be apparent on the chart as work progresses.

INSTRUCTIONS: To make working the interlocking squares easier the chart shows the squares in their entirety. One fourth of the remainder of the panel is charted.

Tape the canvas and place marks for Four-way Bargello (see page 111). Begin working at center—"A" on the chart. Place the small square. Fill in the center with a Smyrna cross stitch. Work Four-way square in all four quadrants. Proceed to the interlocking squares, counting carefully. Observe the over-under effect and maintain this. Complete to outside edge following the chart. Work a row of back stitches between rows of Gobelin stitch, using a single strand of matching yarn.

Block and finish as desired (see page 115).

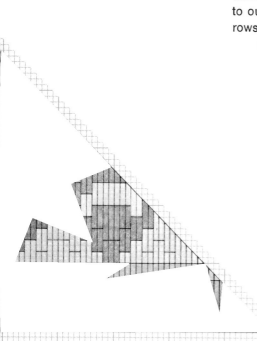

BARGELLO SQUARES PANEL

The little squares that make up the border and center of this delicate panel offer endless possibilities for other uses. Sixteen squares with a narrow Gobelin border would make a fourteen inch pillow; the individual squares can be pincushions, sachets, coasters, or trivets. An eyeglass case or checkbook cover could be made from four worked on a finer canvas to reduce them slightly in size. To illustrate, one alternate color combination is shown as a pincushion with tasseled corners; another as a mini-picture.

COLORWAY #2

COLORWAY #3

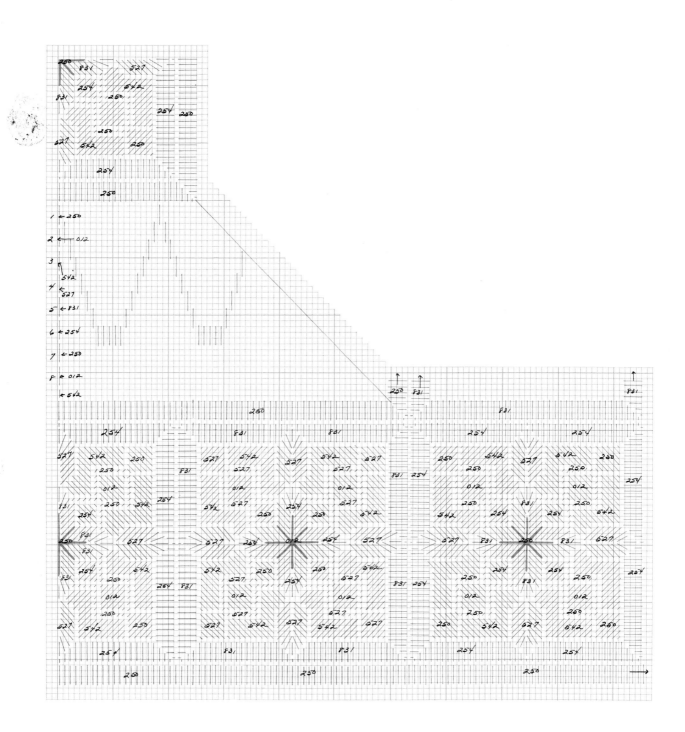

FINISHED SIZE: 16″ x 16″.

MATERIALS:

- #13 tan mono canvas approximately 20″ x 20″.
- #20 tapestry needle.
- Persian yarn as follows: 250, Tea Rose, 2 skeins; 254, Dusty Pink, 2 skeins; 831, Pale Pink, 2 skeins; 527, Moss Green, 2 skeins; 542, Fawn Green, 1 skein; 012, Ivory, 1 skein.

Yarn quantities below are for framed panel or large pillow. Pincushion and picture requirements are 1 skein each color.

- Colorway #2 (Pincushion): 365, Dark Blue, 2 skeins; 385, French Blue, 2 skeins; 395, Light Blue, 2 skeins; 215, Cinnamon, 2 skeins; 257, Light Tan, 1 skein; 020, Natural, 1 skein.

- Colorway #3 (Mini-picture): 113, Dark Brown, 2 skeins; 427, Medium Gold, 2 skeins; 467, Light Medium Yellow, 2 skeins; 545, Avocado, 2 skeins; 843, Fireball, 1 skein; 853, Flesh, 1 skein.

- One-half yard appropriate fabric for pillow back.

NOTE: Separate yarn and work with two-ply throughout.

STEP: The flame pattern in the inner border is a 4-3 step. There is no regular step for the square motifs.

INSTRUCTIONS: A first glance at the chart makes the panel appear more difficult to work than it really is, as it was necessary to show the layout as well as the alternating colors of the border squares. Construction is not difficult if the center square is worked first; followed by the inner border, which is an easy flame pattern repeating all six colors; and finished with the squares completed one at a time to form the final border.

Tape the canvas and mark for Four-way Bargello (see page 111). The miter lines are needed for the inner border and are also handy reference points as the square designs are placed.

One-quarter of the center square is diagramed, but since it is exactly like the border square shown in full at lower right of the chart, it is easier to work from the full diagram. The square is best worked in the following order: Work the pale pink flower motif over the marked center of the canvas. Add the eight long stitches indicated by the heavy lines on the chart. Work the leaves, noting their position in relation to the tips of the petals. Outline the square, beginning with the Gobelin stitch over a single thread at the tip of one leaf. Fill in spaces within square, with the pattern stitches as laid out on the chart.

With color 250, Tea Rose, work one row of Gobelin stitch over four threads around square. The next section of the chart shows only one row of the flame pattern to the miter line. The numbers and stitches shown at the left side indicate the subsequent rows and the colors in order of use. Begin with Row 1 in color 250 at the center of the panel and follow the chart to the miter line to establish the pattern. Attach the yarn at the center and work to left miter line, duplicating pattern established to right line. Work subsequent rows in the color order indicated, completing the pattern to the miter lines as the rows grow longer.

If desired, the rows of the flame pattern can be worked round and round the entire square rather than in the individual sections, as is usually recommended.

Outline the completed inner border with a row of Gobelin stitch worked over four threads in color 250. Beginning on the center line with color 254, outline a square as the chart indicates. Work complete square before proceeding to next. If inner sections of panel have been counted correctly, five squares will fit exactly on each side edge. Finish panel with a row of Gobelin stitch worked over four threads in color 250.

ART NOUVEAU PANEL

This is one of my favorite pieces. What makes a designer favor one work? Is it the way in which stitch direction combines with the flow of color from the center of the inner square? Is it the quilted look of the overall design? Perhaps it is the glowing combination of rusts and greens. Or is it the way a small portion of the design is repeated in slightly different form in each of the three sections? Is it the interesting outer border, or the art nouveau feeling that evolved as the design took shape? It is probably a total of all these reasons, for this piece reveals to best advantage designer's hallmarks—a completely original method of design development and a careful, sensitive use of color.

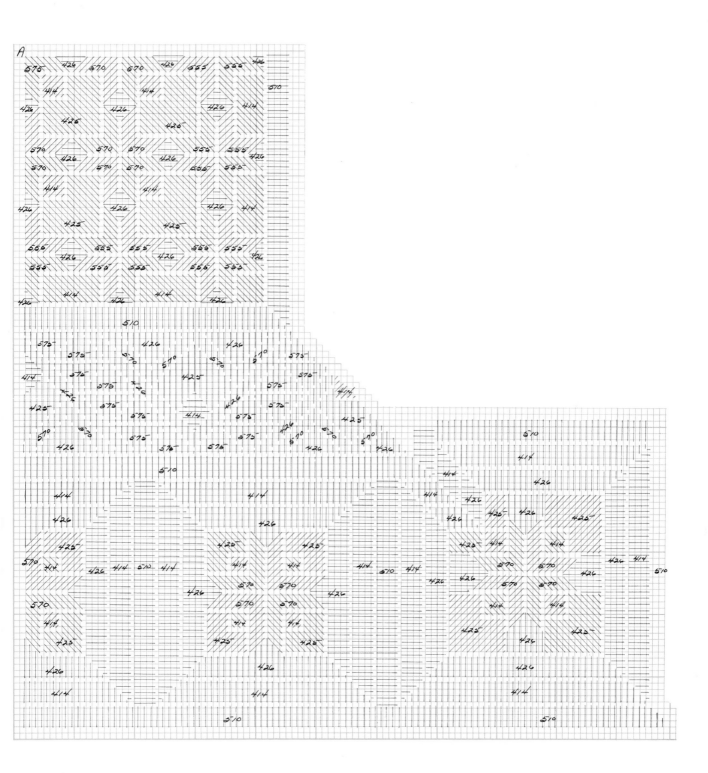

FINISHED SIZE: 15″ x 15″.
MATERIALS:
- #14 white mono canvas approximately 19″ x 19″.
- #20 tapestry needle.
- Persian yarn in the following colors: 510, Medium Green, 2 skeins; 555, Green Giant, 1 skein; 570, Celery Leaf, 1 skein; 575, Spring Pea Green, 1 skein; 414, Rust, 2 skeins; 426, Medium Rust, 2 skeins; 425, Indian Pink, 1 skein.

NOTE: Separate yarn and work with two-ply throughout.
STEP: Since the design is not a typical Bargello pattern the step is not regular. Stitch length and step for each is apparent on the chart.

INSTRUCTIONS: Tape canvas and mark for Four-way Bargello (see page 111). Although the piece is not worked as such, the miter lines are handy reference points as the work progresses. Before starting to work, read paragraph about this group of charts on page 113.

Work out from the center, starting with palest green "star," which should be centered over the intersection of lines on the canvas that is indicated by "A" on the chart. Next work the eight "stars" surrounding the center one, noting that the points of each "star" always share a mesh with those of the adjacent one. Add a third row of "stars" in the next deeper shade of green. The square now contains five rows of five "stars" each. Fill in open spaces with rusts, following the chart for stitch direction for lower right quadrant only. Turn chart to work remaining sections so that the long stitches always slant toward the center—or run parallel to the miter lines. When working the crosswise stitches between the "stars" reach under the end green stitches and work the rust underneath so no canvas shows through.

Work Gobelin border around square and follow with the inner border, which is worked best beginning at the center of one of the sides. Work another Gobelin border around this section.

Outer border is again best worked beginning at the middle of one of the sides. Work each square individually. Note slight variation in the corner squares. Gobelin border surrounds entire outside edge of piece.

Work a row of back stitch with a single strand of yarn in matching color between rows of Gobelin stitch.

Block and frame as shown or make up into a pillow (see page 117).

MATERIALS FOR BARGELLO

Bargello is a specialized form of canvas embroidery that uses basically the same materials as other forms of needlepoint. However, since Bargello incorporates features and problems that are uniquely its own, some tips and pointers about materials can make purchasing them easier.

Of utmost importance in all the materials is good quality. The time invested in every embroidery effort is its single most expensive ingredient, and this should be kept in mind when materials are purchased. Not only do good yarn and fine canvas contribute greatly to the pleasures of embroidery, they are also easier to use and produce a product worthy of the time involved.

The beginner should never be misled into purchasing poor materials on which to learn and experiment. More often than not the experience discourages all future efforts. This is not to intimate that one must have only the most expensive supplies, however. Seek a happy medium in a shop or department store that stocks a wide range of good materials and take advantage of the knowledge of the salespeople there.

THE CANVAS

As with needlepoint, the foundation for Bargello is canvas. Made from either cotton or linen threads, this familiar fabric has an open weave of mesh or squares into which the stitches are worked. There are two distinctly different weaves of canvas. Either type is suited to Bargello embroidery, depending upon personal preference.

The top piece of canvas shown on page 96 is mono canvas. As its name indicates, it is woven so that one horizontal and one vertical thread cross at each intersection. This results in an open weave that is easy to see and accommodates the Bargello stitches very nicely.

The other drawing shows the weave of Penelope canvas. Inspection reveals that the warp and weft threads are in pairs and that each intersection of the canvas is formed by four interlocking threads. This makes a very stable canvas. Note that the vertical threads are placed close together, while a small space separates the horizontal pairs. Because of this weave Penelope has a definite "up and down" grain, and should always be worked with the selvage edges at the sides of the piece so the Bargello stitches will fit most closely together.

MONO CANVAS

PENELOPE CANVAS

Another good Bargello canvas that is not shown is a recent development called interlocking mono. At first glance it looks much like mono, but inspection reveals that like Penelope the warp and weft threads are in pairs. The pairs are closely entwined and interlock at the intersections to impart to the canvas the advantages of both the other canvases—a good firm weave plus an open, easy-to-see mesh.

All three types of canvas come in white, cream, and ecru. Color will not affect the quality, but should be chosen with the colors that will be used in the embroidery in mind. If the colors of the Bargello will be predominantly pastel or light, white is the best choice. Darker colors look best on ecru canvas, since there is less contrast between the colors of the yarn and the tiny specks of canvas that show when the embroidery is finished.

Canvas is available in many sizes, the size being determined by the number of mesh per inch. This number is the name given to the size. Thus #10 canvas has ten mesh per inch, #14 has fourteen, etc.

The sizes of canvas that produce the best Bargello are those ranging from ten to seventeen mesh per inch. Fourteen is probably the most universally preferred, as it is small enough to allow for a reasonable amount of detail but at the same time is not so fine that it takes forever to complete a design.

The pieces in this book use a wide range of canvas sizes, but concentrate most heavily on #14, for the reasons above. Some small projects are worked on fine canvas, in the hope that the reader will enjoy the experience and venture into others also using the small mesh. For beginners and those who love bold design there are also pieces on #10 canvas. There is no "best" size for Bargello. The stitches and designs will work out beautifully on a variety of sizes. The choice of canvas size should be based on the finished effect desired.

Choose canvas carefully and reject any that have an excess of irregularities. Threads that run thick and thin will cause uneven stitches. Knots are weak spots that will affect the wear of the completed work. The canvas should feel smooth to the touch, and the threads should be round rather than pressed flat. The sizing or stiffening of the canvas is important also. The canvas depends on the sizing to maintain its shape, but there should not be an excess of the material on the threads. The best canvas will be firm and crisp, but not stiff and rough.

Because of the way the Bargello stitch lies on the canvas, the selection of canvas is particularly important, and as one becomes more proficient in the embroidery it increases in importance. Sometimes the selection process seems almost erratic, for what seems like a canvas that meets all the necessary criteria in the shop will not be appropriate at all when the stitches are actually worked. The stitches may not look smooth no matter how much care was used in working them, or the canvas may hold them so far apart that the threads show through. For this reason when one finds a good canvas it is wise to lay in a stock for future use. Price does not seem to be a factor in this problem—it is simply the weave and the thickness of the threads.

Another canvas problem that is not apparent until the Bargello is completed is that often it is not truly even-weave. The number of threads is probably correct, but in the finishing process the canvas was pulled slightly out of "square." The result is that a pillow top planned to be fourteen inches square may turn out to be fourteen by fifteen, even though the number of stitches in each direction is exactly the same. This can be very annoying and is another good reason to keep a stock of excellent canvas when you find it.

THE YARN

One of the greatest pleasures in working Bargello is watching the design grow as the colors interact with each other. The large and growing popularity of all needlework has led manufacturers to market yarns in a variety never before known. Finding the colors and precise yarn for any project is now a pleasure instead of a seemingly endless search. Persons who are far from a city need only consult a catalogue, and those in town have a choice of many specialty shops. Informed salespeople are on hand in most shops to assist those not certain of their needs. In short, shopping for materials for a Bargello project is fun and choosing yarn will be exciting. Families of yarn with as many as six values are offered to make the delicate shadings of Bargello possible. Bright contemporary colors that almost sing have been added to the traditional colors, so that there are many selections to appeal to every taste.

Persian yarns are among the most versatile and widely used needlepoint yarns. These yarns are especially adaptable to Bargello. Because they are three-ply with a slight twist, they can be used for various sizes of canvas by separating the ply. Used as they come from the skein, they cover #10 and #12 canvas well. Two strands of the three-ply yarn are fine for #13, #14, and #17 canvas. A single strand can be used on the very fine petit-point-sized canvas.

Despite their softness, Persian yarns are sufficiently long wearing to be practical for most Bargello projects, even chair seats and other upholstery. Most have been moth-proofed and are colorfast. Learn to read the labels as yarn is purchased. Most manufacturers have gone to a great deal of trouble to put pertinent information on the label; often a lot of time or a costly mistake can be avoided simply by reading it carefully.

One important fact that is found on the label is whether the yarn has a dye lot number. If it does, it is better to purchase enough to complete a project at one time. Dye lots do vary slightly and though in many Bargello pieces these variations can be concealed, it is much more desirable not to have to bother with the problem.

The projects in this book have been worked primarily with Persian yarns. Each project lists the exact yarn used, the color numbers, and the quantities used. This is done to assist the reader in purchasing supplies that will duplicate the items exactly, not with the aim of advertising or recommending a particular product. The yarn quantities given are based on Columbia-Minerva's 25-yard pull skein. The color numbers, unless otherwise noted, are for either Columbia-Minerva or Paternayan Persian Yarns. It is hoped that this system will simplify purchasing. Naturally other yarns can be used, provided they cover the canvas well, and color substitutions can be made.

NEEDLES, THIMBLE, AND FRAMES

The instructions for each project specify the exact size needle that should be used. This is the familiar tapestry needle, with an elongated eye and a blunt point. These needles are available in small packages, and it is wise to keep several on hand. The package containing an assortment of sizes makes certain the right needle is always available when a new project is started.

A pair of good embroidery scissors is a valuable accessory. Reserve them for use only on needlepoint, and keep them in a case so that they will not accidently damage the work when it is stored.

Many people feel that any work done with a needle requires a thimble. However, there are also many who find using a thimble clumsy, and cannot become accustomed to one. Beautiful embroidery can be worked with or without a thimble. The choice is purely personal.

Whenever any type of needlepoint is discussed, there is always much talk about whether a frame is necessary or not. There are advantages to both using a frame and not using one. Like the use of a thimble, it is a decision the individual will have to make. Bargello does not stretch the canvas out of shape, and really does not require the use of a frame. To put it on a frame makes it less portable. Also, when the canvas is on the frame it is necessary to work with one hand above and one below the frame. Each stitch then becomes two operations instead of one. The use of the frame will, however, maintain the canvas in its original new condition, with all the threads straight and true. It is probably best to try it both ways and then decide.

THE STITCHES

Bargello is one of the most popular of the canvas embroideries. One factor contributing to this popularity is the easy-to-master stitch that covers the canvas so quickly. Basically it is a long upright stitch covering a multiple of threads and lying parallel to the vertical threads of the canvas foundation. It seems incredible that this simple stitch could create the beautiful and intricate patterns of Bargello.

UPRIGHT GOBELIN STITCH

Bargello is based on the upright Gobelin stitch and variations in the manner in which it is placed on the canvas. When worked across the canvas in rows, it creates a strong horizontal line. The stitch length can vary according to need; stitches sewn over two to six threads are the most practical. This stitch is widely used in this book as a device for creating border patterns.

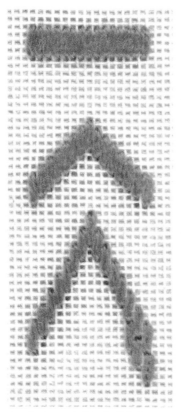

TOP—UPRIGHT GOBELIN
MIDDLE—4–1 STEP
BOTTOM—4–2 STEP

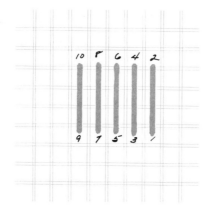

BRICK STITCH

The brick stitch is the upright Gobelin again, this time arranged so that the stitches are alternately two threads up and two down, creating the "brick" pattern. Because it is another upright stitch, it fits well into many Bargello designs. This is an easy, quick stitch that forms a textured but unobtrusive background for busy patterns. The Heraldic Pillow on page 4 makes good use of this stitch to set off the small figures in the design.

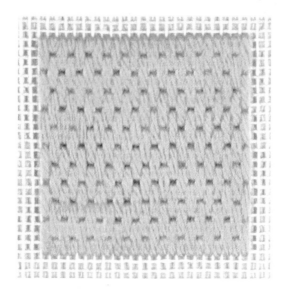 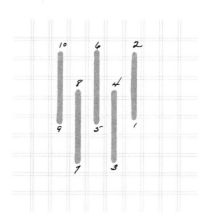

BARGELLO STITCH 4-1 STEP

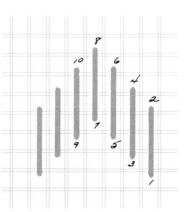

Bargello designs are created when the stitches are placed so that they move up or down the canavs in rows. When the stitches are four threads long and placed one space above or below the last, the arrangement is called a 4-1 step. As the chart shows, this forms a line of compact stitches with a gentle diagonal slope.

BARGELLO STITCH 4-2 STEP

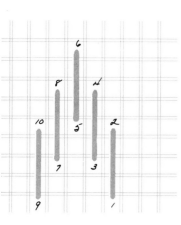

Similarly, when the stitches are four threads long and placed two threads above or below the last, the line is referred to as a 4-2 step. This placement results in a narrower line with a steeper slant. It follows, then, that a pattern in which the stitches move up or down at a rate of three threads will be called a 4-3 step. The line thus formed is one with an extremely sharp peak.

The stitch charts show only the first row of stitches. The second row is worked exactly like the first, with the stitches placed immediately below those of the row above. The top of each stitch of the second row shares a mesh with the bottom of the stitch above. To illustrate this placement the first three stitches of the second row are shown in the photograph of the 4-2 step.

DIAMOND EYELET STITCH

The diamond is a constantly recurring part of Bargello designs, and this eyelet stitch is a natural for filling in areas when something other than the upright Gobelin stitch is needed. It provides a light texture and a change in stitch direction that heightens interest. When more than one eyelet is to be used it is best to work all in the same stitch sequence so all match. Only the odd numbers are shown on the chart, since all even numbers would be in the center, where all stitches share the same mesh.

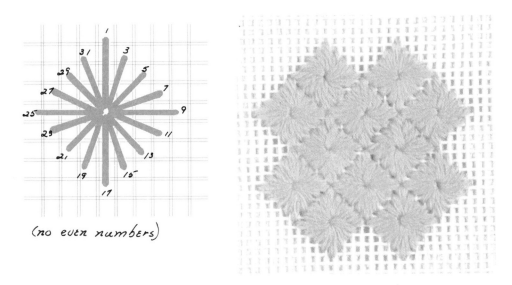

(no even numbers)

SMYRNA CROSS STITCH

This stitch is actually a cross stitch with an upright cross worked on top of it. The result is a raised stitch that fills a square space very neatly. Often the little bit of texture provided by this stitch is just what is needed in a design. Work the stitch in the sequence noted by the numbers on the chart, completing each cross before going on to the next.

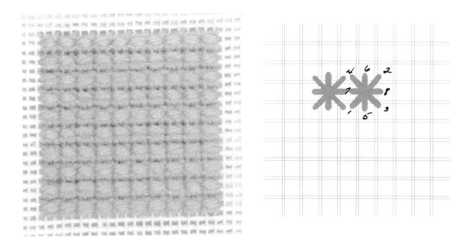

TENT STITCH

The tent stitch is the basic needlepoint stitch, and is probably familiar to all. It is included here as one of the stitches that combines successfully with the Bargello stitch. An area worked in tent stitch will be flatter than the surrounding Bargello stitches, and therefore it is an effective accent.

To be certain that all canvas is covered in the areas where the tent and Bargello stitches meet, work the tent stitches right up to the very edge of the long Bargello stitches and place stitches under the edge of the last row. Do this by lifting the Bargello stitches and working the tent stitches underneath.

The Continental and Basket Weave Stitches

Both the continental and basket weave stitching methods have been diagramed. Since neither the Bargello nor the basket weave causes much distortion of the canvas, it is preferable to use this combination whenever possible.

CONTINENTAL STITCH

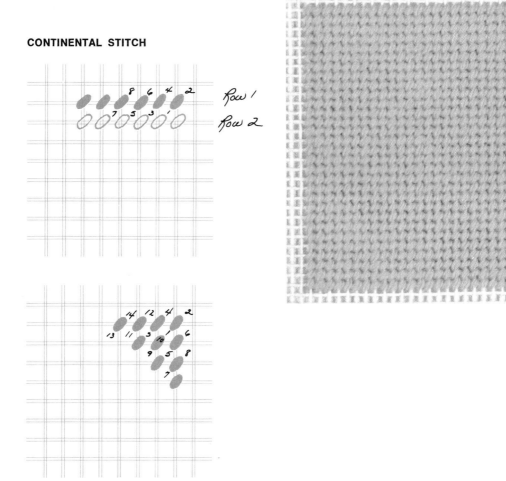

BASKET WEAVE STITCH

EMBROIDERY STITCHES

For special effects it is interesting to add embroidery stitches to some Bargello designs. Several pieces in this book have adopted this technique, and for that reason the stitches used are diagramed here.

Back Stitch

The back stitch is a handy outline stitch that can be worked effectively on canvas to create a curved line. It is invaluable as a covering for the annoying little white specks of canvas that show between even the most perfectly worked rows of Gobelin stitch. It is also a highly attractive addition to the Gobelin rows, for it adds to their appearance by giving them a raised look. It is used extensively in this manner in this book.

Outline Stitch

Another stitch that produces a thin line, the outline stitch, can be used like the back stitch to hide any canvas showing between rows of Gobelin. It will look like a raised cord rather than the flat seedlike back stitches. Use also as an embroidery stitch on top of tent stitch to simulate curved lines not possible with the needlepoint stitch.

Satin Stitch

The satin stitch is worked on canvas exactly as it is on fabric. It can be padded or plain, depending on the depth desired. The stitch can be added on top of existing tent stitch or can be worked on the open canvas as needed. If the stitches are worked directly on the canvas, work the adjacent needlepoint stitches as close as possible to the satin stitches to avoid any canvas showing.

French Knot

French knots are very useful little accent stitches. A solid cluster can fill an area completely, and a single knot can provide a raised focus on a point in the design.

There is of course a vast reservoir of stitches available to the embroiderer—both canvas and free embroidery stitches. This selection has been limited to those necessary to the completion of the projects illustrating this book. It is hoped that after working a collection of these the reader will be inspired to begin designing original pieces, and will draw on other stitches to achieve special effects.

GENERAL WORKING INSTRUCTIONS

Since Bargello is a form of needlepoint, a general knowledge of the basics of that embroidery is helpful, but not essential. Although this book is not intended as a beginner's manual, the charts, instructions, and stitches can be followed by an inexperienced embroidress. The two very easy pillows (pages 2 and 25) can be an introduction to both traditional and Four-way Bargello.

Follow the instructions given with each project. These have been individually written to insure success with every venture. These directions refer the reader to other sections of the book for specific instructions on marking canvas, stitches, etc.

Count the Bargello stitches carefully, following the given chart, until the pattern is established. Accuracy is essential, for very often a line or lines delineate a pattern and all other rows merely follow. If a mistake is made in the first row it will carry into all subsequent rows. Do not waste time trying to work around an error. The more effort one puts into trying to work around a mistake the worse it becomes.

Since Bargello stitches are long, they use up yarn quickly, and it is possible to work with a longer strand of yarn than is generally used for other needlepoint stitches. A length of fifteen to sixteen inches is usually comfortable. More would be awkward to handle, and would cause the yarn to wear thin before it was used.

Learn to work the Bargello stitches with a light, even tension. The stitches lie upright on the canvas and must be loose enough to allow the yarn to "fluff out" and cover the canvas. If the canvas threads are visible between the stitches, either the stitches have been worked too tightly or the yarn is not of sufficient bulk for the canvas. Try stitching with a lighter tension. If that does not solve the problem there are several methods of increasing the bulk of the yarn. Separate the strands of yarn, removing the twist. If coverage is still lacking, give the yarn a steam bath by placing it in a collander over boiling water for three to five minutes. This usually adds enough loft or fluff to cover the canvas. If all else fails, add an additional ply to the number being used. The extra yarn may be necessary in only certain colors—darker colors are sometimes noticeably thinner than their counterparts in the same brand. Use whatever method is needed to cover the canvas completely.

A waste knot, which is removed when its purpose is served, is a very good device for fastening the first stitches on a new canvas. The knot is placed on the right side of the canvas about two inches from the position of the first stitch. As subsequent stitches are worked, the long strand on the back will be fastened and the knot can then be cut away.

Begin and end other strands by weaving them into the stitches on the wrong side of the work. Since Bargello stitches are so long and loose, it is wise to weave ends back farther than for other needlepoint stitches. Clip all ends short to prevent their tangling and being drawn through to the right side with other stitches, causing a mixture of colors.

Bargello stitches should lie flat on the canvas with no twisting of the yarn on the right side of the embroidery. Take time to guide the yarn into a perfect stitch every time. The smooth, even surface that results enhances the beauty of the Bargello designs.

If during the working the yarn becomes twisted, hold the canvas up and let the needle swing free. It will unwind itself. Not only is it more difficult to work with a twisted strand of yarn, the work will not be smooth and the yarn will not cover the canvas.

Many Bargello designs depend heavily upon delicate shadings of color that are difficult to differentiate under artificial light. Avoid making mistakes by sorting and marking colors in daylight. The yarn can be loosely knotted into a skein to which an identifying tag is pinned or stapled, or it can be placed in individual plastic bags with the numbers attached. Any system that keeps the shades or values from being confused is fine.

A good embroidress is extremely particular about the care of the canvas both while it is being worked and when it is put away. The piece should be rolled, not folded, and protected to insure that the sizing holding the threads in place is not broken. Stitches placed on threads that are not in alignment will not be as straight and true as they should be.

The work should also be kept as clean as possible. It is a shame to have to have a piece dry-cleaned before it can be made up. There is nothing quite like the new, fresh look of an embroidery that has been well kept during the working.

Never leave a mistake in a piece of Bargello. It is always the first thing the embroiderer will see after the work is finished, even if it is never noticed by anyone else. Far better to rip it out and correct it as soon as it is discovered.

Of course it is always best to buy all the yarn that is going to be needed for a project at one time, but needleworkers are apt to change ideas after a project is begun and may run short of a color of yarn. When this happens it is best to save five or six strands of yarn to match when shopping. The color is easier to duplicate in the hand than after it has been stitched onto the canvas. Also, the change in the reflected light on the stitches causes a slight alteration in color.

The strands can also be helpful if the exact dye lot of the old yarn is no longer available. When the ply is separated and combined with one or two ply of the new dye lot for several rows, the transition from one to the other is hardly noticeable.

An error in marking the canvas in preparation for working Bargello can be very confusing, especially when a second, corrected line is added. An effective method of removing the inaccurate line is to cover it with typing correction fluid. This handy liquid dries quickly, making it possible to begin working almost at once.

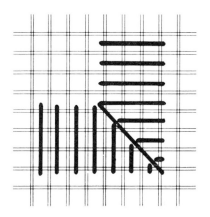

To turn the corner of a Gobelin stitch border neatly, work as shown in the accompanying chart, placing a long diagonal stitch over the line where the stitches meet. The stitches shown are worked over four threads, but the principle applies to stitches of any length. The finished effect is both tidy and attractive.

Rows of Gobelin stitch tend to have rows of tiny canvas specks showing between them, no matter how carefully the stitches have been worked. This problem is inherent in the upright stitches, but to the perfectionist they are very annoying. A row of back stitch worked with a single strand of yarn in matching color between the Gobelin rows covers the exposed threads very effectively. At the same time the little back stitches make the Gobelin rows seem to be raised a little above the rest of the embroidery—a very nice look.

Four-way or Mitered Bargello is one of the most exciting and challenging aspects of needlepoint. When the canvas is divided into four triangles and the design worked out from the center in four directions, the simplest Bargello lines make intriguing patterns. The mitered designs require more skill and thought than the average Bargello, but once the mechanics are mastered these patterns are within the scope of the average needleworker. As a first experiment it is good to try a design like the one on page 25 (Beginner Pillow), which is developed from a continuous line. This type of easy model allows for exploration of the changes that occur at the miter lines when the rows meet, and forms a good understanding of the basics of Four-way as well.

When possible it is best to begin working a Four-way design at the center of the canvas, progressing outward, while keeping the design within the confines of the miter lines. It is necessary to make adjustment in the length of some of the stitches along the miter to form a neat line. The chart for each project shows this in detail. In many cases when a stitch of the length used in the design would leave a single thread along the miter, a longer stitch has been substituted. This avoids working over one thread, making a stitch that usually does not lie flat. Occasionally, however, when it is important that a color be carried up to a sharp angle, the neat stitch is sacrificed for better color placement.

Although it is always best to begin a design in the center of the canvas, there is no absolutely definite order in which the balance of a piece must be worked. Whatever method produces the best Bargello with the least effort is best, and this can vary from person to person as well as from design to design. While one person may prefer to work each section completely before beginning the next, another might embroider the center portions of all four sections and work outward on all four quadrants at the same time. The instructions suggest the best working method for each specific piece, but these can be freely changed at the reader's preference.

Accuracy is the key to success in duplicating designs like those in this book. Work carefully, checking often. An error in the placement of just one stitch can prevent combined patterns from fitting together as they should.

Beautiful neeedlework of any type does not just happen. It is a combination of good design, excellent color, craftsmanship, and attention to detail, put together with patience and love. It will last for many years, so take time to do it right, then be justly proud of it.

THREADING THE NEEDLE

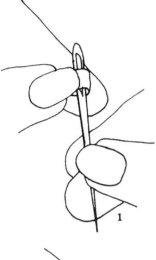

Shown on the accompanying drawing are two methods of threading a needle with yarn. There is another simple but seldom described method that is also entirely correct. Press the end of the yarn tightly between the thumb and forefinger of the left hand. With the other hand force the eye of the needle over the yarn as it is held tightly. The yarn will fit right into the eye with only a little practice.

The paper method is always successful, even with yarn that tends to split and fray. Any of the three techniques is good. Never wet or twist the yarn to insert it into the needle.

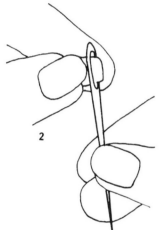

FOLD METHOD

1. Hold the needle between the thumb and forefinger with the eye facing you. Fold the yarn across the eye of the needle and pull tightly to form a sharp fold. Hold the fold firmly and gently withdraw the needle.
2. Force the fold through the eye of the needle.

PAPER METHOD

1. Cut a small piece of paper about an inch long and narrow enough to fit through the eye of the needle. Fold the paper as shown on the drawing and place the cut end of the yarn into the fold.
2. Pass the folded end of the paper through the eye of the needle and the yarn will be carried through easily.

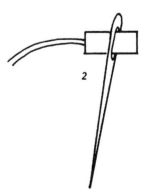

PREPARING THE CANVAS

When a project is planned, a two-inch border of empty canvas should be allowed on all sides of the piece. This is not, as it might at first seem, a waste of canvas, but an essential and functional border that helps maintain the shape and makes blocking easier. A skimpy border is a costly economy. Small projects may require only an inch-wide border, but most do need the full two inches. The estimates of canvas requirements for individual projects in this book include allowance for borders.

Always tape the cut edges of the canvas with masking tape to prevent fraying and to keep the yarn from snagging on the stiff threads as the Bargello is being worked. Use only *masking tape;* other tapes work loose or leave a sticky deposit on the canvas.

Choose markers that are to be used on needlepoint with care. Many new ones are made especially for use on canvas; others for general purposes are waterproof when dry. Always test a marker, regardless of its label, by writing on a scrap of canvas, allowing it time to dry, then soaking it in water. A marker that is going to bleed will then do so on the scrap of canvas rather than on the stitches of a finished Bargello piece.

Avoid using markers in black and other dark colors, for they tend to show through light colors of yarn. Pink, pale blue, orange, and yellow are good choices. The lines need be only dark enough to be seen. Pencil is not generally used for marking needlepoint, but in an emergency it can be used for Bargello with success. Bargello does not get a lot of handling, so the marks are not likely to be rubbed off. Use a #3 pencil, but wield it lightly.

It is very important that Bargello designs be centered on the canvas. The lines needed for centering are so quickly drawn before any work is started that marking the canvas becomes a habit.

CHART #1—DIVIDING CANVAS FOR FOUR-WAY BARGELLO

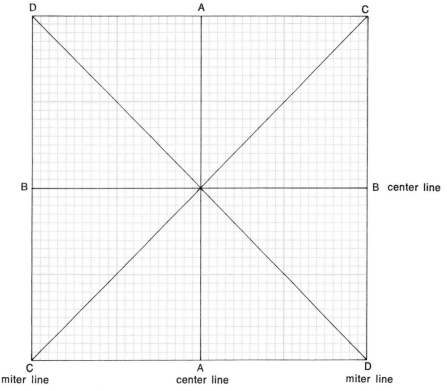

x denotes center mesh or square

CHART 1

This diagram represents a canvas with the four guidelines used in making most of the projects in this book. Lines "A" and "B" dividing the canvas into four quarters are needed for any Bargello design. Lines "C" and "D" are the miter lines necessary for Four-way Bargello. Some designs need only two lines; others need all four. The instructions with each project indicate which lines are necessary for its completion.

Chart 1 shows a piece of canvas with the four lines needed for many of the projects in this book. Lines "A" and "B" are needed for the traditional method of working Bargello (rows all the way across the canvas). Lines "C" and "D" are the miter lines necessary to Four-way Bargello. Some projects will require only "A" and "B"; others will need all four.

To mark the canvas, fold it into quarters and mark the center mesh ("X" on both charts). Open canvas flat and draw lines "A" and "B" so that they cross at the marked square. Draw the lines between two threads so they appear as dots on the cross threads. The two diagonals "C" and "D" must be drawn carefully thread by thread to insure accurate placement. Do not attempt to use a straight edge for this task. Although it sounds painstaking, it takes only a few minutes to place the lines.

Begin at the corners of the center mesh and move diagonally outward, placing a dot on the threads as illustrated in Chart 2. Dots need be only dark enough to be a guide.

Some of the designs need the miter lines only for the borders, but it is best to put all marks on the canvas before the work is begun. This way no stitches hide the center mesh, and the new canvas lies flat ready for the marks.

CHART #2—PREPARING THE CANVAS

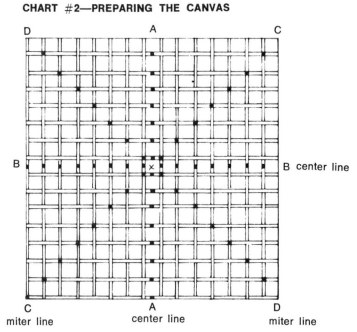

x denotes center mesh or square

CHART 2
This is an enlarged drawing of the center of a canvas on which the four guidelines have been drawn. The lines shown are the same as those on Chart 1 and are identified with the same letters. Note that the lines appear as dots on the canvas.

MAKING THE BEST USE OF THE CHARTS AND INSTRUCTIONS

Two distinct kinds of graphs are included in this book. Both are very easy to use.

The color charts are probably the easiest ever devised for Bargello embroidery, re-creating as they do the needlepoint itself, in very graphic detail. To use these charts count the squares within the inked oblong and make a stitch over the corresponding number of canvas threads. Color placement is indicated by hues as close as possible to those of the yarn, except when the colors are so closely graded that true duplication would make differentiation difficult. These shades have been slightly modified to separate the rows. Colors are always keyed to the yarn numbers immediately below the chart so that there is no confusion. Following the chart is further simplified by cues in the instructions as to the best working method for each individual piece. Every effort has been made to ascertain that the reader will be able to follow the instructions to duplicate the pieces shown.

The color charts are singularly successful when all the stitches are the typical upright Bargello. The inclusion of slanted and horizontal stitches as in some of the designs creates a drawing exercise that cannot be carried out clearly on the color graphs. Rather than exclude these designs, another type of chart has been used. It is different, but not harder to follow.

The black-and-white chart is drawn on graph paper, with each grid line representing a canvas thread. The stitches are duplicated by lines lying over the grid exactly as the stitch lies on the canvas. In other words, if an inked stitch crosses four grid lines, the yarn should be worked over four threads. The yarn should slant exactly like the inked stitch.

A glance at one of these charts will reveal that the method of drawing creates a black-and-white pattern that duplicates the design on canvas. Color numbers superimposed on the blocks of stitches indicate yarn to be used for each area. Again the individual instructions for each piece offer keys to aid in the working of the design.

The materials needed for each project are listed. Canvas requirements include allowances for unworked borders. The best needle size is noted. See page 97 for additional information on yarns used. Substitutions are possible where colors can be duplicated—yardage per skein must be considered when changing from one product to another.

The yarn quantities suggested are based on careful working habits. Some allowance has been made for differences in individual working methods, but it should be noted that the amounts given are really a guide for purchasing yarn. There are stitching methods that differ from mine that use tremendous quantities of yarn—the work is almost double thickness. Naturally, such deviation from the instructions will result in yarn shortage.

When a design is shown in several color combinations, the colors are always listed in the same order to make substitution easy. In other words, the first color in the first colorway should be replaced with the first color in variations #2 and #3, etc.

Specific finishing instructions are included when needed. Since there are so many pillows in the book, a separate section (page 117) deals in detail with their construction.

BLOCKING

Since most of the stitches used in Bargello are upright ones that do not stretch the canvas, you may be happily surprised to finish working and find that your piece needs very little blocking. It is nice to make this discovery, but no matter how neat the finished piece looks, blocking will improve it. This will often make the difference between the "homemade" and the "hand-crafted" look.

Pieces that are still in their original straight condition can often be finished with only the application of a little steam. This can be accomplished with a steam iron if caution is used. Lay the Bargello face down on a heavy towel on the ironing board. Hold the iron just above the surface of the needlepoint and let the steam penetrate the yarn. Do not allow the iron to rest on the needlepoint. This will flatten the stitches, and may distort their shape. Leave the steamed piece in position on the board long enough to cool and dry. In many cases the Bargello will be fully refreshed by this treatment, ready for finishing or mounting.

More often than not, the finished Bargello will be only slightly out of shape but will look rumpled and handled. Such pieces need more than simple steaming to make them look new again. To block professionally, you will need a blocking board—an old drawing board, doiley blocker, or builder's composition board. New devices to make blocking easy are on the market and really do help. If you intend to do much blocking you might want to investigate these aids.

You will also need a supply of rustproof tacks. Even though you are not going to place the tacks into the Bargello, there is always the possibility that a tack could rust and the rusty water seep along the canvas threads into the yarn and stain it.

Remove the masking tape from the edges of the canvas. Mark the center of each side border with permanent ink or a scrap of yarn. Draw the outline of the finished measurements of the piece on the blocking board. Also mark the centers of the sides of the drawing.

Wet the needlepoint thoroughly by rolling it in a wet towel and leaving it several hours or overnight. The effect of this wetting is to soak the yarn and the canvas equally and make the piece easier to stretch. When the needlepoint is removed from the wet towel it should be very limp. The sizing in the canvas has softened. When dry it will again be crisp and new looking.

Do not wet needlepoint by holding it under the faucet. That much water is unnecessary and will only lengthen the drying time.

Match the marks at the centers of the sides of the Bargello to those on the blocking board. With the needlepoint face up, place a tack at each of the four points. Pull if necessary to make the marks match. Working outward from these four points, place a tack every inch until the entire piece is fastened down. It may be necessary to retack some points before the piece is straight, but the needlepoint will remain wet long enough for this to be done. Stubborn pieces may require what seems like a great deal of pulling to straighten them, but usually the canvas is strong enough to tolerate this. The finished needlepoint is actually a very strong fabric.

When the needlepoint has been tacked to the board in a straightened position, it should be left to dry. Care should be taken to dry it in the horizontal position away from heat and sun. Weather conditions will affect drying time, and it is usually a good idea to leave the piece on the board twenty-four hours after it feels dry to the touch. If removed from the board before thoroughly dry, the needlepoint will revert to its unblocked shape.

It is not possible to stretch a piece to a larger size by blocking, nor is it possible to "hold in" a piece to a smaller size. This makes planning doubly important.

Blocking will not remove mistakes in the stitching. It does, however, have the effect of smoothing out the work so that mistakes are not quite so apparent. Best not to depend on blocking to correct—rectify mistakes as soon as they are discovered.

If the needlepoint is placed right side to the board during blocking, the stiches are pressed flat. When the piece is blocked face up, the stitches are rounded and softer. It is a matter of personal preference.

The price of blocking is often included in the price of finishing an article when it is done professionally. This service is usually fairly expensive, so every embroiderer should at least experiment with blocking to understand what is involved. It is not difficult, and it is definitely worthwhile.

CONSTRUCTING A PILLOW

Materials needed for making up a pillow are: appropriate fabric; cable cord (a soft white cord from the drapery department); polyester fiber filling or a pillow form one inch larger than needlepoint in both dimensions; matching thread. Use zipper foot on the machine for best results.

Trim unworked borders of blocked needlepoint to ⅝″. Using this as a pattern, cut fabric backing to same dimensions.

Measure cable cord to one inch longer than the total of lengths of all four sides. Cut an inch-wide bias strip as long as the cable cord. This bias strip can be pieced if necessary. With right side out, fold the bias strip in half, with cord inserted into fold. Stitch as close as possible to cord.

With the needlepoint right side up, pin the finished cording along the edge of the last row of stitches, raw edges on the same side as the edges of the needlepoint piece. Clip the cording at the corners so a square turn can be made. Overlap the ends of the cording, leading them toward the raw edges of the needlepoint. Machine stitch in place.

Place fabric for back on a flat surface right side up. Position Bargello on top with the wrong side up. Pin layers together, then sew, stitching on the line of stitches holding the cording in place. Leave bottom partially open to receive filler.

Trim seams and corners. Turn right side out. Fill with loose polyester fiber or a purchased pillow form. Slip stitch to close opening.

MAKING YARN TASSELS

Tassels are a luxurious finishing touch for many needlepoint items. They can be made of one accent color or a combination of the colors in a piece. The length and thickness can vary to suit any project, but all are made simply.

Cut a piece of cardboard as wide as the desired length of the tassel. Wind the yarn around the cardboard as many times as necessary to achieve the thickness wanted. If you are making more than one, count the number of times the yarn encircles the cardboard so all will be of uniform size.

Cut a length of yarn (approximately 12 inches, depending on the size of the tassel). Double it and slip it under the yarn on the cardboard. Tie firmly at the top of the tassel. Leave the ends of this piece of yarn to attach the tassel to pillow.

Slip the yarn off the cardboard. Tightly wrap another length of yarn around the tassel about half an inch below the tie. Leave the ends of this strand long enough to trim with the bottom edges. Cut bottom loops of tassel. Trim to a neat edge, including the ends of the tie.

INDEX